revelation of Revelation

AN URGENT MESSAGE FOR THE CHURCH

VOLUME 6
THE NEW JERUSALEM

*The Fourth Narrative
of
Revelation*

Rev 21:9-22:21

The Naked Apostles
Phil and Colleen Livingston

Published by: The Naked Apostles

WAUCONDA, IL

Phil and Colleen Livingston/The Naked Apostles
304 Barrington Road
Wauconda, IL 60084
www.nakedapostles.org
email: info@nakedapostles.org

Ordering Information:
Quantity sales. Special discounts are available on quantity purchases by corporations, associations, and others. For details, contact via email or the address above.

revelation of Revelation, *An Urgent Message for the Church* Volume 6: The New Jerusalem/The Naked Apostles, Phil and Colleen Livingston.
ISBN-978-0-9960102-9-0

Table of Contents

Chapter 1: The Fourth Narrative..1

Chapter 2: The New Jerusalem 13

Chapter 3: The River of Life 29

Chapter 4: The New Temple Area..45

Chapter 5: Jesus is Coming..86

Bibliography..89

About the Authors..91

This book is dedicated to the Father of all creation. May the mercies He has bestowed upon us be infinitely remembered and celebrated through the eternity of eternities now and forevermore.

Amen

He who overcomes will inherit these things, and I will be his God and he will be My son.

— Revelation 21:7 New American Standard Bible

Volume 1

Introduction to Revelation

Volume 2

The Seven Letters of Revelation
1:1-3:22

Volume 3

The Seven Seals of Revelation
The first narrative of the vision
4:1-11:18

Volume 4

The Main Characters of Revelation
The second narrative of the vision
11:19-16:21

Volume 5

The Fall of Babylon and the Church Corrupt
The third narrative of the vision
17:1-21:8

Volume 6

The New Jerusalem
The fourth narrative of the vision
21:9-22:21

CHAPTER 1

The Fourth Narrative

T his is the fourth and final narrative of the book of Revelation. It is by far, the shortest. For all intents and purposes, the third or previous narrative (*Volume 5*) brought a decisive and clear conclusion to the contents of the scroll. The plan of judgment and redemption (the contents of the scroll with seven seals) has been completely revealed from beginning to end. It had ended with a moving, but direct personal message from the Father, whose plan it is. If Revelation had ended with *Volume 5* (the third narrative) it could be considered a complete body of work. However, to make the book utterly comprehensive, as is the Hebrew meaning of the number 4, the Lord saw fit to dedicate a fourth narrative to the New Jerusalem and life everlasting. This is not a narrative whose focus is concerned with the process and unfolding of the plan of judgment and redemption, rather it centers around the destination of the redeemed, and the role the New Jerusalem has during the 1,000-year reign of Christ and after.

The previous narrative had ended with the New Jerusalem and how it transcended the 1,000-year reign of Christ, surviving the destruction of planet earth and the universe on the Day of Judgment. After the dead are judged, John sees the New Jerusalem come down before the judgment seat and the sheep who are found worthy to enter into the next world. The previous narrative ended with these verses (below) which were before the Father spoke His words to every individual:

Amp Rev 21:1 THEN *I saw a new sky (heaven) and a new earth, for the former sky and the former earth had passed away (vanished), and there no longer existed any sea.*

Amp Rev 21:2 *And I saw the holy city, the new Jerusalem, descending out of heaven from God, all arrayed like a bride beautified and adorned for her husband;*

Amp Rev 21:3 *Then I heard a mighty voice from the throne and I perceived its distinct words, saying, See! The abode of God is with men, and He will live (encamp, tent) among them; and they shall be His people, and God shall personally be with them and be their God.*

Amp Rev 21:4 *God will wipe away every tear from their eyes; and death shall be no more, neither shall there be anguish (sorrow and mourning) nor grief nor pain any more, for the old conditions and the former order of things have passed away.*

Amp Rev 21:5 *And He Who is seated on the throne said, See! I make all things new. Also He said, Record this, for these sayings are faithful (accurate, incorruptible, and trustworthy) and true (genuine).*

The New Jerusalem is the only thing on earth besides the redeemed that survives the destruction of the natural universe. The natural universe, in its entirety, is thrown into the lake of fire on the Last Day. However, the New Jerusalem was never made of natural matter, nor did it have its origins from earth. From its beginning, it was constructed of heavenly or supernatural matter. In the case of the redeemed it is a little different. They died to their body made of natural matter and receive a new celestial body made of supernatural matter. Nothing made of natural matter makes it into the new world where there is life eternal. The mortal human race has become extinct.

The starting point of this narrative is a vision of the New Jerusalem, having been constructed in heaven awaiting its descent to the earth. It comes complete with its own mountain to sit on. This narrative, that has the New Jerusalem as its subject, goes backwards from where the previous narrative ended, overlapping it. Does this skew the timeline of the narratives? Just as in the previous cases, no. The visions and story of one narrative are complete where it's story ends. This new narrative is just that; a new narrative or story with its own beginning because it has a different emphasis or subject. In fact, this is a common occurrence in the style Revelation was written in. When one story of a vision or subject matter ends, the next vision starts at the beginning of its subject; naturally overlapping the timeline of the other. So again, although each vision and narrative keep their own timeline in a linear way, the different visions within the narratives naturally overlap each other because they are telling the same story from the perspective of a different aspect.

When we write a story, we tell it once, and typically break it down in chapters and say in those chapters everything that pertains to the full story at that part of the timeline. Then, move forward to the next chapter as the timeline progresses. However, Revelation is best told and understood when the full story is told in light of one aspect, then when complete, tell the full story again from a different aspect or according to a different focus. With all four narratives being told with their different emphases, it creates a more holistic and detailed account of the overall story.

In writing the book of Revelation this way it is much easier to acertain details of certain aspects when the whole story is told in light of that particular aspect. That is as opposed to trying to glean details concerning one aspect or another from the story being told once. This is the literary style the visions and book of Revelation are outlined with.

The last subject on the overall timeline of the book of Revelation would naturally follow to be the destination of the redeemed; those who survive or transcend the complete annihilation of everything (judgment). Those who transcend the extinction of the mortal human race are those mortals who metamorphize into celestial humans gaining a body constructed of spiritual matter (this is redemption). In addition to the redeemed, are the New Jerusalem and the mountain it sits on, which together will have been on the earth for 1,000-years previous to the Last Day. How does the New Jerusalem survive the destruction of the universe? The reason is because it is a city that never was made up of natural matter.

It is natural matter which is destroyed when the earth and the entire universe, along with every element that comprises them, that is destroyed and melts in the lake of fire while spiritual matter goes on, unaffected.

2Pe 3:10 But the day of the Lord will come like a thief. The heavens will disappear with a roar; the elements will be destroyed by fire, and the earth and everything in it will be laid bare.

"Everything," That is to say, everything that is clothed with a body comprised of the elements of the natural universe. Peter is referring to "everything" that has a spiritual nature to it, in addition to its body of flesh. Specifically, he is referring to animals who are spirit and natural flesh and particularly natural humans, who not only have a body of flesh but spirit and a soul. It is they who will be "laid bare"—caught unclothed, naked without a body at this event.

Humans are made up of three different natures; spirit, soul, and body. Two of those natures are spiritual, not natural. When the Last Day comes, every element of the natural universe will melt into the lake of fire including the natural body of man. Suddenly, after a loud crash; the earth, the universe, and the fabric of space will be gone. However, the human being will be left bare as Peter tells us above. That is, in the sense that the earth below one's feet will be no more, and just as suddenly, neither will his physical body. He will be a soul, unclothed without a body of any sort. The spirt and soul of the man will remain intact. That is except for the fact it is disembodied—lacking an outward manifestation to express itself or interact with its environment. This is what will occur on the Last Day!

After this happens and every living thing is dead (disembodied), the disembodied souls, being held in the realm of the dead since the first man died, together with those who lost their natural body when the universe melted, will all be resurrected in order to face judgment. Meaning, to be given a body to clothe their disembodied souls with in order to face God and be judged.

It will be a body comprised of spiritual matter, not physical matter (elements) because the natural elements which a physical body are comprised of, are no more—they are extinct. Then, as a result of the consequence of how each individual conducted themselves in the body, and given they are found unacceptable, they will be thrown alive into the lake of fire. This time it will be their spirit, soul and resurrected body, unlike the residence of Hades who were confined as a disembodied soul. In the lake of fire, the entire man will not only be confined, eternally separated from God, but tormented constantly, unable to escape his prison—ever.

This is called in the Bible, "the second death." They died once losing their natural body becoming a disembodied soul and spirit, then alive again, resurrected with a spiritual body, only to be thrown alive while clothed with their resurrected body into the lake of fire. This is the same fate as the Devil and his fallen angels, some of who are in prison in the abyss (the bottomless pit) of Hades, held over for their final destination in the lake of fire on the Last Day.

Note: When humans die, they become disembodied and are held in that disembodied state, in the realm of the dead, in Hades. For them to face judgment and to experience a second death, they have need for another body since they are in a state of disembodiment. Nimrod was a hybrid of the spiritual and natural, and was a giant of a man with superhuman strength. However, in all that he still was clothed with a natural body of flesh. He died and is currently held captive in the abyss of Hades (a place reserved for supernatural creatures[angels, demons, hybrid giants and such]) in a disembodied state as all men who die. However, he will, in the near future, walk the earth again. In order to do so, a body will be constructed for him made of the body parts of sacrificed dead humans by the false prophet in the Jewish temple (yet to be constructed).

We read in Revelation that the Devil himself will be chained and confined into the abyss of Hades, and after 1,000-years he will be "released" (not resurrected) and allowed to influence the mortal humans on the earth. It also tells us that on several occasions the Devil releases dreadful spiritual creatures from the abyss allowing them to kill and torment the mortal humans on the earth.

Nimrod, the giant who had a natural body and died, has need of a new body in order to escape the abyss and walk the earth once again. This, however, is not the case for the Devil when he is to be released out of the abyss in order to walk the earth. The reason being is the Devil has a celestial body, not a natural body; only natural bodies die. Nimrod is prisoner in the abyss in a disembodied form. The Devil will be held prisoner in the abyss while embodied with his celestial body.

Both spirit and spirit embodiment cannot be destroyed, this is why evil spirits and evil spirit beings must be confined for eternity. This holds true in the case of the corrupt human spirit and the evil souls of humans, but not for their body made of natural matter. That dies and decays as all natural matter will. However, on the Day of Judgment the disembodied human souls will all be given a resurrected body made of spiritual matter. Those who suffer the second death of being thrown alive (embodied) into the lake of fire will then have a spiritual body that cannot be killed.

Laws of Thermodynamics:

Energy exists in many forms, such as heat, light, chemical energy, and electrical energy. Energy is the ability to bring about change or to do work (to be animated/ alive). Thermodynamics is the study of energy.

First Law of Thermodynamics: Energy can be changed from one form to another, but it cannot be created or destroyed. The total amount of energy and matter in the Universe remains constant, merely changing from one form to another. The First Law of Thermodynamics (Conservation) states that energy is always conserved, it cannot be created or destroyed. In essence, energy can be converted from one form into another.

The Second Law of Thermodynamics states that "in all energy exchanges, if no energy enters or leaves the system, the potential energy of the state will always be less than that of the initial state." This is also commonly referred to as entropy. A watchspring-driven watch will run until the potential energy in the spring is converted, and not again until energy is reapplied to the spring to rewind it. A car that has run out of gas will not run again until you walk 10 miles to a gas station and refuel the car. Once the potential energy locked in carbohydrates is converted into kinetic energy (energy in use or motion), the organism will get no more until energy is input again. In the process of energy transfer, some energy will dissipate as heat. Entropy is a measure of disorder: cells are NOT disordered and so have low entropy. The flow of energy maintains order and life. Entropy wins when organisms cease to take in energy and die.[1]

There is a difference between the first death and the second death:

The first death: is the death of the natural body. The body dies and the human spirit and soul of the man live on remaining conscious of itself. When the human mortal body dies, the man (now disembodied) lives on, but is severed from his mortal body. It matters not what the body suffers or endures after its death. That is because the human soul has no connection to it and does not experience its decay or the mutilation of it, for example.

It is like when a limb gets severed from the body. Once separated, you can do whatever you will to that severed limb and the individual will feel no pain or sensation whatsoever. Likewise, the soul is free from whatever happens to that body, even if it is cremated by fire until it is reduced to a pile of ashes. The soul will feel no pain or sensation from the burning of his body, even though he is consciously aware. However, that's not to say that being in a disembodied state doesn't have its own types of agonies, it does!

The second death: Since after experiencing the first death the disembodied soul is given a resurrected body comprised of spiritual matter that cannot be killed, it seems ironic to call being thrown alive into the lake of fire a "second death" when your second body cannot be killed. Let us examine this: There are three destinations in the realm of the dead, Hades, that we are told of in the Bible. All of which imprison. They are:

1. **The paradisiacal place** known as Abraham's bosom; a place of rest and peace a disembodied soul is held captive in while he awaits his resurrected body and ability to fellowship directly with the Lord in Heaven.

2. **The hellish place** known as hell or Hades where the disembodied soul is imprisoned in a state of torment awaiting his resurrected body which will enable him to face God, be judged, and thrown alive into the lake of fire for eternity.

3. **The abyss** known as the bottomless pit. This was intended for creatures who possess spiritual bodies and are not disembodied. The first two destinations are for the purpose to imprison and isolate the disembodied souls from roaming the earth and influencing the living. The third destination is meant to imprison or isolate those creatures who are not disembodied from roaming the earth and influencing the living. The understanding that the name leaves us with when it is called the "bottomless pit" is a place where a body is in a constant state of falling—never reaching a bottom. To move something, one has to plant his feet on the ground in order to push something from it. It is like trying to push a car in outer space with nothing to stand on while in zero gravity. If one has no footing it matters not how strong he is, he can push against and move nothing whatsoever. So, the spirit being with a (spiritual) body imprisoned in the bottomless pit, the

abyss, can be thought of as being in a constant state of falling unable to move or influence anything whatsoever.

The purpose of these three destinations of which comprise Hades, the realm of the dead, is to temporarily (until the Last Day and the end of the natural universe) confine the dead, the disembodied souls and the imprisoned spirit beings who have spirit bodies from influencing the living on the earth. Likewise, it is to prevent them from attempting to possess the bodies of the living because they themselves no longer have one of their own. And to prevent certain spirit beings from possessing the natural bodies of the living, so they may have expression in the natural world.

The purpose of the lake of fire is to eternally confine the decidedly unredeemable, the indestructible evil spirits, souls and beings (all of which have spiritual bodies) from either influencing or participating in eternity in the spiritual realm—the new heavens and the new earth. Given they are eternal, they need to be in a constant state of flux in order for them to have no chance whatsoever to gain footing, compose themselves, and have effect on anything at any time or anywhere. This is similar to the effect of the bottomless pit where they suffer while being in a constant state of falling. The lake of fire is such a place.

Spirit is energy, life, consciousness and power to move or animate. Since the lake of fire is so hot that it can melt and consume every element in the natural universe, and since energy cannot be destroyed or used up but only be made to change form; then the heat of the lake of fire can burn the spirit being and his spirit body to the point where it is not destroyed but consumed in the heat until it changes form. Alive, but forever and constantly in a state of flux, unable to stabilize in one form or another long enough to take inventory of its own form in order to animate it or have influence over anything whatsoever.

Imagine being burned at the stake. As the heat of the flames consume your flesh changing it from one form to that of ash, you endure the most unbearably excruciating agony possible. However, when it comes to the first death which involves the natural body, it can die from smoke inhalation or breathing in superheated air long before it will die of its burns, and even longer before it completely changes form from flesh to a pile of ashes. When death by smoke inhalation or by breathing superheated air happens, the mind or soul of the man is severed from the body. After that, whatever the body goes through during that process of being burnt by the fire (changing from one form to another) the soul or conscious mind of the man no longer suffers the agony of that process. The living soul or mind of the man is free from any sensation of what his severed and lifeless body is experiencing. There are many stories and movies of how a person does a mercy killing so his friend no longer suffers what his body endures.

However, in the case of the second death where the soul possesses a resurrected spiritual body that does not get severed from it through death, this becomes a different experience all together. In the lake of fire, where the body is being consumed by the heat but is unable to be destroyed. Rather it is in a constant state of being changed from one form into another. That is very much unlike one being burned at the stake whose body dies, finally giving sweet relief as the heat causes the body to change forms from an organism of flesh to a pile of ashes. The soul with a resurrected body does not get free from the agony of that process of changing from one form to another that disembodiment (a severing of the soul from the dead body) would afford. The body is alive and although its form is constantly being consumed by the heat of the lake of fire and constantly changing form, the mind/soul suffers the fullness of the unbearable agony, unable to be severed from the body to be free of the pain and agony, ever!

Now let us look one more time at the irony of being thrown alive into the lake of fire being called, "the second death" when in reality you have a body that does not die. You cannot die in the sense of being unclothed from your spiritual body while it is being forever consumed in the heat of the lake of fire changing form from one state to the other—you cannot be set free through the death of that body or from its constant and eternal all-consuming agony. Instead, you are being consumed in the heat in a constant and forever state of agony and flux unable to escape or be an influence on anything at any time. However, the reality is that in the lake of fire you are in a constant state of dying or death; in that the body is constantly changing form, no longer being what it was just a moment ago. However, in spite of this, you and your body are always alive, never being severed from the body letting the life escape its agony. Therefore, it is not ironic at all but literal for it to be called, "the second death."

Our natural body being burned at the stake gives us a small but brief taste of the lake of fire. While being burnt at the stake, that point of greatest agony lasts but a moment due to the welcomed and sweet relief of being severed from the body through its death, even though it burns on, continuing its process of changing form until it is ashes. In the lake of fire, with an unkillable spiritual body, that moment of welcomed sweet relief due to death of the body never comes, it is never consumed or used up but alive, experiencing its changing of form constantly without getting that relief—no freedom from the agony of the body, eternally. In this way all corruption and everything that would express evil contending with God's order of things, will be confined, never having any affect, expression, or influence in the new heavens or on the new earth.

Note: In the story of Lazarus and the rich man, the description of the rich man in the hellish place of Hades might seem to conflict with what we are saying above. Likewise, there are accounts of people dying or in visions being given a tour (so to speak) of hell bringing us a witness of how terrible it is to be in hell. However, those accounts do not conflict with the description above. They are an account of a different place. The destination of the rich man in Jesus' story and the testimonies of those who descended into hell, then came back to witness what it was like, is not the lake of fire. As horrific as their description of hell is, the lake of fire is immeasurably worse. They are two different places. One is a temporary holding place, the other is a final destination which no one occupies at this time. Hell is a place for disembodied souls who indeed suffer torment in that place until the Day of Judgment when they receive a spiritual body. The other destination is for those disembodied souls who are reclothed with a spiritual body and suffer a second death while being eternally thrown alive into the lake of fire. In fact, Hades, with all three of its compartments will also be thrown into the lake of fire after its usefulness has expired and emptied on the Last Day.

For the same reasons that the spirit and soul of the man remain intact on the Last Day because it is constructed of spiritual matter, the New Jerusalem which was made in the spiritual realm of spiritual matter, along with the mountain that it sits on, will, likewise, not be destroyed when everything in the natural universe is. That is despite the fact it was on the earth as the residence of the Lord, His Father, His army of angels and all the celestial humans who co-ruled the earth with Him at the time every atom in the universe melted.

Because of its material make up, it says in Revelation that although the gates to the New Jerusalem are always open, the corrupt natural being can never enter in. That is because it is not a natural environment for a natural body to survive in.

NRS Rev 21:22 *I saw no temple in the city, for its temple is the Lord God the Almighty and the Lamb. [23] And the city has no need of sun or moon to shine on it, for the glory of God is its light, and its lamp is the Lamb. [24] The nations will walk by its light, and the kings of the earth will bring their glory into it. [25] Its gates will never be shut by day--and there will be no night there. [26] People will bring into it the glory and the honor of the nations. [27] But nothing unclean will enter it, nor anyone who practices abomination or falsehood, but only those who are written in the Lamb's book of life.*

. . . but only those whose names are written in the Lamb's book of life." This statement signifies that it is only those who have become celestial humans may enter in. Given the above statement and that the gates of the New Jerusalem are never closed and nothing unclean can enter in, supports that natural humans or anything evil (celestial or natural) can enter in.

Notes

1 Farabee, Mike (2001). Retrieved December 2019, from Estrella Mountain
    Community College:
    https://www2.estrellamountain.edu/faculty/farabee/biobk/BioBookEner1.
    html

CHAPTER 2

The New Jerusalem

The fourth narrative

The beginning of the vision that tells the narrative of the New Jerusalem starts when the angel, who had delivered the wrath of the seventh bowl, invites John to see the Lamb's bride, the New Jerusalem.

> *WEB Rev 21:9 One of the seven angels who had the seven bowls, who were loaded with the seven last plagues came, and he spoke with me, saying, "Come here. I will show you the wife, the Lamb's bride." ¹⁰ He carried me away in the Spirit to a great and high mountain, and showed me the holy city, Jerusalem, coming down out of heaven from God . . .*

Note: Previously we were told that the city-state called the Roman Catholic Church and great prostitute which sits on the seven hills of Rome, is the "great city" of Babylon who rules the kings of the earth (Rev 17:18). She (the Roman Catholic Church) boasts that she is not a widow and sits as a queen and will never mourn (Rev 18:7). However, we are told by the Lord that she is the bride of the beast and antichrist. Likewise, great in the earth as it is, it is a city made of natural matter, and will be utterly destroyed in the judgment of fire.

NIV Rev 17:1 One of the seven angels who had the seven bowls came and said to me, "Come, I will show you the punishment of the great prostitute . . .

Then later it says:

NIV Rev 21:9 *One of the seven angels who had the seven bowls full of the seven last plagues came and said to me, "Come, I will show you the bride, the wife of the Lamb."*

It is very likely that the same angel who invited John to see the punishment of the great prostitute in the previous narrative is now inviting John to see the New Jerusalem on its mountain. It would stand to reason that this angel who showed John the bride of the antichrist/beast (the Vatican), the *Church Corrupt*, would give hope back to John by showing him the bride of Christ (the New Jerusalem) the *Church Pure*. Nevertheless, in doing so, the angel helps us see the contrasting fate of the two different elements of the Church. The *Church Corrupt* does not last, and the *Church Pure* is everlasting.

Isaiah gives details of this mountain that comes down to the earth from heaven, made of spiritual matter:

The Mountain of the LORD

NAS ISA 2:1 *The word which Isaiah the son of Amoz saw concerning Judah and Jerusalem.*
NAS ISA 2:2 *Now it will come about that In the last days* *The mountain of the house of the LORD* *(the New Jerusalem) Will be established as the chief of the mountains, And will be raised above the hills; And all the nations will stream to it.*

The New Jerusalem (the house of the Lord) sits upon the top of this mountain that comes from the spiritual realm. It will be the highest and most important mountain on the earth at the advent of the 1,000-year reign of Christ. From that mountain the Lord will reside and rule the entire earth and its population of mortal men. The celestial humans, who have been reclothed with bodies of spiritual matter, will not only reside in the Lord's house (the New Jerusalem), but co-rule the mortal humans with the Lord as His ministers.

Currently, Mount Everest is a high and chief mountain. It has a glory which men behold it with, and they risk their lives to ascend it. When the mountain of the Lord arrives it will have a spiritual, as well as a majestic, eternal, and authoritative glory, of which on top, the light that illuminates the sunless earth will emanate from.

NAS ISA 2:3 And many peoples will come and say, "Come, let us go up to the mountain of the LORD, To the house of the God of Jacob; That He may teach us concerning His ways And that we may walk in His paths." For the law will go forth from Zion And the word of the LORD from Jerusalem.

This (above) is referring to the sovereignty of Christ during His 1,000-year reign from the New Jerusalem on its mountaintop.

Nebuchadnezzar's dream speaks of the mountain the New Jerusalem sits on:

NIV Da 2:32 The head of the statue was made of pure gold, its chest and arms of silver, its belly and thighs of bronze,
NIV Da 2:33 its legs of iron, its feet partly of iron and partly of baked clay.
NIV Da 2:34 While you were watching, a rock was cut out, but not by human hands. It struck the statue on its feet of iron and clay and smashed them.
NIV Da 2:35 Then the iron, the clay, the bronze, the silver and the gold were broken to pieces at the same time and became like chaff on a threshing floor in the summer. The wind swept them away without leaving a trace. But the rock that struck the statue became a huge mountain and filled the whole earth.

The rock not made of human hands, smashes to dust all traces of the Babylonian kingdom in the earth, then the rock grew into a huge mountain. That is because during the great tribulation Jerusalem will become the great city of Babylon, which rules the nations of the earth. That rock is the supernatural invading the natural, beginning with Jesus, the Son of God, then His mountain from the spiritual realm, with the New Jerusalem on top, and His entourage of celestial humans, angels, and His Father.

NIV Isa 10:5 "Woe to the Assyrian, the rod of my anger,
in whose hand is the club of my wrath!

The Assyrian is the rod of God's anger and the club of His wrath that He uses to punish His people during the great tribulation and before. Then, God will deal with His rod,

He will destroy every trace of what He used to punish His spiritually adulterous people. That rod is Nimrod (who is "the Assyrian"), and his kingdom, Babylon.

NIV Isa 14:25 I will crush the Assyrian in my land;
on my mountains I will trample him down.
His yoke will be taken from my people,
and his burden removed from their shoulders

It is there, on Mount Zion, that the transfer of power from the beast (antichrist) to the Lord must take place when the Lord crushes the beast.

NAS ISA 2:4 And He will judge between the nations, And will render decisions for many peoples; And they will hammer their swords into plowshares and their spears into pruning hooks. Nation will not lift up sword against nation, And never again will they learn war. NAS ISA 2:5 Come, house of Jacob, and let us walk in the light of the LORD.

Isaiah (above) continues telling us about the coming mountain of the Lord from which He will live among mortal men and rule the nations from.

Note: As a part of the Lord ruling the mortal humans from atop this holy mountain; the judgment of the 4 horsemen being lifted is referenced here by the Lord in the (above) verses of Isaiah saying He will abolish the power of war, domination, and take men out from under slavery serving the interest of the despotism imposed by Babylon and its beast over the earth. Later in Isaiah (below) he tells us how the power of the other 2 horsemen will be abolished by the Lord as well. Those horsemen that bring to a premature end to 25% of the lives on earth. And how disease and the animal kingdom will no longer be hostile or kill humans.

NIV Isa 65:20 "Never again will there be in it
an infant who lives but a few days,
or an old man who does not live out his years;
he who dies at a hundred
will be thought a mere youth;
he who fails to reach a hundred
will be considered accursed.

NIV Isa 11:8 The infant will play near the hole of the cobra,
and the young child put his hand into the viper's nest.
NIV Isa 11:9 They will neither harm nor destroy

NIV Isa 65:25 The wolf and the lamb will feed together,
and the lion will eat straw like the ox,
but dust will be the serpent's food.
They will neither harm nor destroy
on all my holy mountain,"
says the LORD.

Isaiah emphasizes that the holy mountain with the New Jerusalem atop it will be the chief or highest of all the mountains in the earth.

WEB Rev 16:17 The seventh poured out his bowl into the air. A loud voice came out of the temple of heaven, from the throne, saying, "It is done!" 18 There were lightnings, sounds, and thunders; and there was a great earthquake, such as was not since there were men on the earth, so great an earthquake, so mighty. 19 The great city (Jerusalem, the headquarters of the beast) was divided into three parts, and the cities of the nations fell. Babylon the great was remembered in the sight of God, to give to her the cup of the wine of the fierceness of his wrath. 20 Every island fled away, and the mountains were not found.

In Revelation above, we are told that there is an earthquake so profound that all the cities of the world collapse, which in turn destroy the entire world system; including the infrastructure and the manufacturing of all the cities. The powerbrokers and financial empires lose their control in one fell swoop. Everything is leveled to ground zero with no pieces left to be picked back up, so things can recover and be as they were before.

An entirely new system of government, commerce, class and social structure will need to be instituted. Every island disappears, and the mountains cannot be found. There is so much tectonic plate movement causing this massive earthquake that the mountains drop down raising up the ocean basins while pushing the continents back together. The earth will return to the pre-flood condition (pre-cursed). This would mean that there will be no mountains or hills above the height of 12,000 feet. That is except the mountain of the Lord that the New Jerusalem sits on when it arrives.

Note: If the mountains had been higher than 12,000 feet during the pre-flood days, the flood waters would not have covered them by a minimum of 20 feet, as the Bible told us they had.

Because of this earthquake, the continents will pull back together becoming one land mass. As a result, the oceans will become only one ocean extending from the north of the landmass. Reason being, it is the north where we are told that the coastal people of Gog—Magog will come from after the thousand-years.

WEB Zec 14:4 His feet will stand in that day on the Mount of Olives, which is before Jerusalem on the east; and the Mount of Olives will be split in two, from east to west, making a very great valley. Half of the mountain will move toward the north, and half of it toward the south.

We see in Zechariah this same earthquake described in Revelation. Only where Jesus touches down, it creates a big valley which shifts mountains. The reason this becomes important is because the New Jerusalem, its mountain, and all the saints in their glorified bodies are following Jesus to the earth. Also, verse 5 tells us when Jesus creates this valley, it will be used as a highway for everyone who lives there to escape before the New Jerusalem touches down with all the celestial humans. This is an amazing scene in and of itself, everyone fleeing to get out of the way of this huge city as it descends out of heaven down to the earth. A new authority is definitely coming to the earth to make all things new, which demands that the systems of the past be utterly torn down! It will be a different world to live in, during the reign of the Lord.

WEB Zec 14:5 You shall flee by the valley of my mountains; for the valley of the mountains shall reach to Azel; yes, you shall flee, just like you fled from before the earthquake in the days of Uzziah king of Judah. Yahweh my God will come, and all the holy ones with you.

The "holy ones" coming with Jesus are the celestial humans which either received their celestial bodies when:

- The 144,000 whom Jesus set free from Hades receiving their celestial bodies and are called the first fruits of His redeeming work.

- Those who never tasted death because they gave up their lives in the body in order to be one with Jesus in union with Him. And therefore, received their celestial body before the head of their natural body hit the ground in death.

- Those who either died or suffered through the great tribulation without coming off their testimony of Christ, taking the mark of the beast, or worshiping the beast. Those who died during that time period of 3-1/2 years will become disembodied, go to Hades, and be raised from the dead being given a celestial body along with those living that stayed true to their profession of faith and are caught up in the sky lining up behind the Lord, all poised to come back on the earth soon after. This will happen as part of the end of the 3-1/2 years of God pouring out His wrath on the world/Babylon, which will be in the days right before the seventh and final trumpet blows.

Together, these three groups of people will comprise the holy ones/celestial humans, who will come back to the earth with the Lord and the New Jerusalem for His 1,000-year reign on earth.

Let's take a look at the city that is coming down from heaven, from God.

WEB Rev 21:11 *having the glory of God. Her light was like a most precious stone, as if it were a jasper stone, clear as crystal; 12 having a great and high wall; having twelve gates, and at the gates twelve angels; and names written on them, which are the names of the twelve tribes of the children of Israel. 13 On the east were three gates; and on the north three gates; and on the south three gates; and on the west three gates. 14 The wall of the city had twelve foundations, and on them twelve names of the twelve Apostles of the Lamb. 15 He who spoke with me had for a measure a golden reed to measure the city, its gates, and its walls. 16 The city is square, and its length is as great as its width. He measured the city with the reed, twelve thousand twelve stadia. Its length, width, and height are equal. 17 Its wall is one hundred forty-four cubits, by the measure of a man, that is, of an angel. 18 The construction of its wall was jasper. The city was pure gold, like pure glass. 19 The foundations of the city's wall were adorned with all kinds of precious stones. The first foundation was jasper; the second, sapphire; the third, chalcedony; the fourth, emerald; 20 the fifth, sardonyx; the sixth, sardius; the seventh, chrysolite; the eighth, beryl; the ninth, topaz; the tenth, chrysoprasus; the eleventh, jacinth; and the twelfth, amethyst. 21 The twelve gates were twelve pearls. Each one of the gates was made of one pearl. The street of the city was pure gold, like transparent glass.*

As you approach the New Jerusalem this is what you would see: The walled city of the New Jerusalem is square in shape. It is 12,000 stadia by 12,000 stadia in size, and 12,000 stadia high. That is 1,500 miles wide and 1,500 miles long, and the city is 1,500 miles high. That would mean that there is a gate in the walls of the city every 375 miles on all four sides, given there are 12 gates. At 144 cubits the walls of the city are about 22 stories high. By today's standards, if there is a building which went up as high as the city (1,500 miles) that would mean that building would be 792,000 floors. Perhaps it is the throne of the Father and the Son, which is 1,500 miles high, looking down on the city and the earth. In that case their glory would indeed be what illuminates the New Jerusalem. Likewise, and as it bends and wraps around the world, their glory will also be the light of the world.

Amp Isa 66:1 *THUS SAYS the Lord: Heaven is My throne, and the earth is My footstool. What kind of house would you build for Me? And what kind can be My resting-place?*

And again:

Amp Mk 12:36 *David himself, [inspired] in the Holy Spirit, declared, The Lord said to my Lord, Sit at My right hand until I make Your enemies [a footstool] under Your feet.*

In addition, it must be considered that just as when the earth is relocated into the spiritual realm, it brings with it its own atmosphere (sky) as a part of its body. As a result, if you measured the breadth of the natural earth as an alien object from the natural realm in the spiritual realm, you would: 1) include in your measurement the atmosphere around it, meaning all space its foreign matter would occupy; and 2) make a three dimensional measurement (length, width, and height) so that you include all the space this bubble of alien matter occupies. That would be the full measurement of the earth which enters into the spiritual realm. In other words, the earth goes into another realm with its own bubble made of the same kind of matter from which it comes (the natural universe). That entire bubble of natural matter defines the boundaries of it, and not just the planet earth itself, given it ascends to the spiritual realm made of a different kind of matter.

The same concept would apply to the city, the New Jerusalem. It is a city from one realm descending to the earth made of matter from a different realm. It would need to have 3 dimensional boundaries which define its mass on all sides since it is made of matter from a different dimension. In other words, the New Jerusalem and its "atmosphere" (or the boundaries of its matter [made up of a different kind of matter than where it rests]) extends 1,500 miles high, as well as wide and long.

In addition to that, Isaiah and John told us it comes with its own mountain to sit upon. A mountain which is higher than any mountain in the earth, and it becomes the chief of mountains. The city comes from the supernatural realm with its own base. A mountain base which is as holy as the city, in that it is holy ground and from the heavens where God is.

Just as when the earth makes the transition from the natural to the supernatural dimension bringing with it the sky (its atmosphere), the New Jerusalem will bring with it holy ground from the heavens for it to set on.

WEB Da 2:34 *You saw until a stone was cut out without* (human) *hands, which struck the image on its feet that were of iron and clay, and broke them in pieces. [35] Then was the iron, the clay, the brass* (bronze)*, the silver, and the gold, broken in pieces together, and became like the chaff of the summer threshing floors; and the wind carried them away, so that no place was found for them: and the stone that struck the image became a great mountain, and filled the whole earth.*

Now let's take a moment to take in these measurements. To help give perspective this means the city is 2,250,000 square miles in size. It is said in Biblical prophecy that the current Jerusalem will be the exact location of the New Jerusalem. However, the current Jerusalem is only 48 square miles in size. The New Jerusalem can hold in its space 46,875 of the current city, Jerusalem, inside its walls. In fact, the entire nation of Israel itself is currently only 8,000 square miles, 263 miles long and between 9 miles at its most narrow point, to 71 miles at its widest point. You could fit 281 nations of Israel inside the walls of the New Jerusalem. To give a better idea of how big the New Jerusalem is, take the mainland of the United States (not including Alaska); from the eastern border of Illinois continuing south along the eastern border of the state of Mississippi down to the gulf of Mexico, then every state west to the Pacific ocean is the approximate size of the "city," the New Jerusalem.

Now consider this, Israel is currently bordered by two seas. The Mediterranean and the Dead seas. This is why it is only nine miles wide at its narrow point. The size of the mountain top needed to hold the city must be, not only bigger than the city's footprint, but its base must be enormously larger to support its top. Next, this could explain the nature of this huge earthquake because the topography of the earth would have to completely change just to make room for the mountain and the New Jerusalem atop it to sit between the two seas. However, we are told, the two seas remain part of the landscape of the earth during the 1,000-year reign of Christ.

WEB Zec 14:8 It will happen in that day, that living waters will go out from Jerusalem; half of them toward the eastern sea (the Mediterranean Sea)*, and half of them toward the western sea* (the Dead sea)*; in summer and in winter will it be.*

In fact, it says that because the river of life, which originates from the New Jerusalem, flows into the Dead Sea, it will become a freshwater lake teeming with life:

NIV Eze 47:8 He said to me, "This water flows toward the eastern region and goes down into the Arabah, where it enters the Sea. When it empties into the Sea (the Dead Sea)*, the water there becomes fresh.*
NIV Eze 47:9 Swarms of living creatures will live wherever the river flows. There will be large numbers of fish, because this water flows there and makes the salt water fresh; so where the river flows everything will live.
NIV Eze 47:10 Fishermen will stand along the shore; from En Gedi to En Eglaim there will be places for spreading nets. The fish will be of many kinds—like the fish of the Great Sea (the Mediterranean Sea).

We see that where there is currently only nine miles between the two seas, now must become 1,500 miles plus to accommodate the New Jerusalem and its mountain base. Is the massive earthquake that happens when Jesus touches down going to rearrange the earth in a way that makes room for the New Jerusalem to plant itself?

WEB Rev 16:18 There were lightnings, sounds, and thunders; <u>and there was a great earthquake, such as was not since there were men on the earth, so great an earthquake, so mighty. 19 The great city</u> (Jerusalem, the headquarters of the beast) *<u>was divided into three parts, and the cities of the nations fell.</u> Babylon the great was remembered in the sight of God, to give to her* *the cup of the wine of the fierceness of his wrath.* <u>*²⁰ Every island fled away, and the mountains*</u> <u>*were not found.*</u>

WEB Zec 14:4 *His feet will stand in that day on the Mount of Olives, which is before Jerusalem on the east; and the Mount of* <u>*Olives will be split in two, from east to west, making a very great*</u> <u>*valley. Half of the mountain will move toward the north, and half of it toward the south.*</u>

We are told that there will have never been an earthquake as massive as this in all of human history. Is it possible to suddenly rearrange the earth in such a fashion? And how violent must this earthquake be that it would be greater than any earthquake previously in the history of man? Let us explore this statement:

Amp Rev 12:15 *Then out of his mouth the serpent spouted forth water like a flood after the woman, that she might be carried off with the torrent.*

Amp Rev 12:16 *But the earth came to the rescue of the woman, and the ground opened its mouth and swallowed up the stream of water which the dragon had spouted from his mouth.*

Let us keep in mind that earthquakes and tectonic movements were so great at the time the flood waters covered the earth, that it separated land masses into continents while shoving up mountain ranges to amazing heights which created ocean basins big and deep enough to contain the flood waters so there might be dry land for the human race.

Currently, the earth's highest mountain reaches 29,035 feet above sea level. The deepest depths of the oceans reach down approximately 36,200 feet. Geologists who are also Creationists have done the math to understand what would happen if all the mountain ranges were pushed down proportionately (as a whole) so that the highest peaks were lowered to a height of 12,000 feet. This movement would likewise force the ocean basins to shrink in size and for the bottom of their floors to rise up. There findings were that it would push the continents together and lift up the ocean floors resulting in the water levels of the oceans to rise and cover all the dry land over 20 feet higher than the highest mountain (at 12,000 feet).

Genesis 7:24 tells us that from the moment the flood began, there was 150 days or 5 months before the waters finished draining off the land into the newly formed ocean basins. 40 of those 150 days the flood waters continued to rise covering the highest mountains by a minimum of 20 feet; thereby leaving the waters with nowhere to go. That left exactly 3 months and 20 days for both a place to be created for the waters to recede into, and for the waters to finish draining off the land into those places.

Picture the violence required that in the course of 3-2/3 months (110 days) there was tectonic plate movement and earthquakes so violent it separated the land into continents by:

- Breaking apart the land, pushing the parts away from each other and up
- Creating the distances between them that they currently are
- Creating bigger mountains and more mountain ranges
- Increasing their heights so that the highest peaks become almost 20,000 feet higher than previous to the flood
- And finally, creating basins that would allow all the flood waters to recede into, creating dry land.

WEB Mt 17:20 "*. . . For most certainly I tell you, if you have faith as a grain of mustard seed, you will tell this mountain, 'Move from here to there,' and it will move; and nothing will be impossible for you.*

In answer to our questions above that ask if the earth can be reshaped in such a manner and how violent does an earthquake have to be in order to be the worst? We know how bad earthquakes can be, considering what happened to create dryland after the flood, as described above. In lieu of the reshaping of the topography that happened to the earth as a result of creating dryland after the flood; we are told by the Bible that when Jesus returns there will be an earthquake so violent that never has there been one to match it. How can we reconcile that being the case at the flood, no other earthquake could match the one that happens as a part of the Lord's return considering what happened as a part of the flood?

NIV Rev 16:18 . . . *No earthquake like it has ever occurred since man has been on earth, so tremendous was the quake.*
NIV Rev 16:19 *The great city split into three parts, and the cities of the nations collapsed*

NIV Rev 16:20 Every island fled away and the mountains could not be found.

NIV Rev 16:21 From the sky huge hailstones of about a hundred pounds each fell upon men. And they cursed God on account of the plague of hail, because the plague was so terrible.

WEB Zec 14:4 His feet will stand in that day on the Mount of Olives, which is before Jerusalem on the east; and the Mount of Olives will be split in two, from east to west, making a very great valley. Half of the mountain will move toward the north, and half of it toward the south.

The violent earthquakes that created the high mountains and ocean basins happened over the course of 3 months and 20 days. The earthquake that happens when Jesus returns is a single event that rocks the whole world and levels all the cities of the earth. This earthquake basically undoes what happened to create dryland after the flood.

Another aspect is the height of the city being 1,500 miles high. Here are a few facts to get an idea of what that looks like. The Willis Tower (formerly, the Sears Tower in Chicago, IL.) at 1,729 feet tall (almost .3 of a mile) was, in its day, the tallest manmade building. Mount Everest is 29,000 feet tall, which is about five miles higher than sea level. Commercial jets cruise at 39,000 ft. That is 7.4 miles high. The end of the earth's atmosphere is about 75 miles high. This is the decided border between sky and outer space called the "Karman line." The space shuttle is designed to operate between 115 miles up to a maximum of 596.5 miles. The space station is 190 miles up, and the Hubble Telescope is a whopping 370 miles up in outerspace. Lastly, the moon is 238,900 miles away from the earth.

To give a more practical idea, a mortal person would start having minor difficulties breathing starting at about 6,500 feet above sea level (that is a little over 1 mile high). For example, Denver, Colorado, where the city is nick named "the mile high city," the air is thin, and visitors have a little trouble breathing until they become accustomed. Water boils at 200 degrees Fahrenheit in Denver as compared to 106 degrees on Mount Everest, and at 213 degrees at sea level. A space suit is required to survive at 6.8 miles high.

Lastly, concerning the height, the mountain will be the highest point on earth. Then you must add another 1,500 miles of height for the New Jerusalem, which makes the earth rather lopsided. Surely this would normally present problems when it comes to the physical laws the earth is subject to in the natural universe. However, the earth will have already been transported from the natural universe to the spiritual realm before the New Jerusalem comes down to the earth for the reign of Christ. It will be a physical object with its physical atmosphere in the spiritual realm which is made of different matter. Additionally, an object, the city the New Jerusalem and its mountain made of supernatural matter, will pierce the physical atmosphere made of natural matter and rest on the physical earth. Then the supernatural will interact with the natural for 1,000 years. God will make His home among mortal men, and the earth will indeed be His foot stool, just as the prophets said.

NIV Rev 21:3 And I heard a loud voice from the throne saying, "Now the dwelling of God is with men, and he will live with them. They will be his people, and God himself will be with them and be their God.

Next, you can see the Willis Tower (the Sears Tower) from 46.5 miles away while walking towards it. Say a crowd of people were to go on a pilgrimage to the mountain of the Lord, if the city, the New Jerusalem, were only 300 miles tall you could potentially see it from 1,500 miles away, as you were walking towards it on the ground.

It says a constant stream of people will come to the mountain of the Lord from all the nations of the earth during His reign. Let's say you started out on a pilgrimage to the New Jerusalem, to praise Him bringing gifts and offerings. Furthermore, on your journey you got as close as New York City is to the coast of Los Angeles. Conceivably, you would see the city on the horizon. You would see the city rising up as if it reached the moon, depending where on the horizon the moon was sitting (in reality there may not be a moon at this time because the earth has passed into the supernatural realm from the natural universe).

Conversely, if the moon (the earth's satellite) is included in the bubble of the natural realm which is ingulfed by the spiritual realm, that would mean that the bubble of natural matter the physical earth extends over 238,900 miles. Furthermore, the bubble of spiritual matter, which is 1,500 miles high, would be completely engulfed within the bubble of natural matter (which is in turn, ingulfed in spiritual matter). It would be kind of like the boundaries of an egg yolk that is fully within the white of an egg, whose boundaries are fully within the shell of an egg. The egg yolk would represent the New

Jerusalem made of supernatural matter and its boundaries within the natural earth and its natural environment; the egg white would represent the earth and the boundaries of its physical environment; finally the egg shell represents the boundaries of the spiritual realm that the egg white is within.

> WEB Rev 21:22 *I saw no temple in it, for the Lord God, the Almighty, and the Lamb, are its temple.* ²³ *The city has no need for the sun, neither of the moon, to shine, for the very glory of God illuminated it, and its lamp is the Lamb.* ²⁴ *The nations will walk in its light. The kings of the earth bring the glory and honor of the nations into it.* ²⁵ *Its gates will in no way be shut by day (for there will be no night there),* ²⁶ *and they shall bring the glory and the honor of the nations into it so that they may enter.* ²⁷ *There will in no way enter into it anything profane, or one who causes an abomination or a lie, but only those who are written in the Lamb's book of life.*

You would see the towering city, which seemingly goes on forever, both horizontally and vertically. The walls are made of the beautiful stones described above. However, the colors of the walls would be so surreal they would look alive—like living colors— even as if they are breathing. They would not look like jasper as we know it because first of all, it will be so pure that it will be translucent, clear as a crystal. Next, light would not be reflecting off of it but coming out from it.

NIV Isa 60:2 *See, darkness covers the earth*
and thick darkness is over the peoples,
but the LORD rises upon you
and his glory appears over you.
NIV Isa 60:3 *Nations will come to your light,*
and kings to the brightness of your dawn.

NIV Isa 60:19 *The sun will no more be your light by day,*
nor will the brightness of the moon shine on you,
for the LORD will be your everlasting light,
and your God will be your glory.
NIV Isa 60:20 *Your sun will never set again,*
and your moon will wane no more;
the LORD will be your everlasting light,
and your days of sorrow (the great tribulation) *will end.*

Light will stream out from above the city and even up, over, and through the walls like a flood of water. This will be the light that illuminates the whole world. It may be like walking into the sun. That is with the exception that it will not be the kind of light that blinds because of its brilliance, but brilliant light which causes everything to be illuminated. Meaning, with the nature of the light the Lord provides, there will be no shadows and it will not seem as the light is coming from a single direction and reflecting off of things for us to see. All things, indoors and out, will be illuminated by the light which comes from the city. It will seem as if light comes out from inside all things.

However, it will still look like you are walking into the sun itself when you walk towards the city of the Lord. It will be as Isaiah said (above), as you get closer to it in your pilgrimage, it will be like a dawning of the sun. As you travel towards it, at first, its light will crack the horizon. The closer you get, the higher in the sky the light streaming out of the New Jerusalem will be until you arrive at the base of the holy mountain. Then its light will be spilling over the walls, coming down like a water fall from almost directly above you, like the noon day sun.

CHAPTER 3

The River of Life

The River of Life

> *WEB Rev 22:1 He showed me (the) river of (the) water of life, clear as crystal, proceeding out of the throne of God and of the Lamb, 2 in the middle of its street. On this side of the river and on that was the tree of life, bearing twelve kinds of fruits, yielding its fruit every month. The leaves of the tree were for the healing of the nations.*

The tree of life bears 12 kinds of fruit 12 times a year. The number 12 is an important number in Hebrew, meaning government. There are 12 patriarchs, 12 tribes, and 12 apostles. The Lord once told the Apostles that He is the vine or trunk and they are the branches which would bear much fruit.

In Hebrew symbolism, trees are another word for leaders. However, to refer to "trees" as representing leaders, and to call that usage of the word "trees" a symbol does not, in the Hebrew language, fully or truly describe that usage as we would understand a symbol. It is, in fact, how their language works. The Hebrew language uses tangible objects to define or describe conceptual things. Using an example we have used before in this study: When the Old Testament states in translation that a person was angry, the Hebrew word used in the original language reads that the person was "nose." That is because when someone is angry their nose flares up. The word "anger" is an intangible concept. Conversely, a nose is an object that when flared it is tangible then likewise, it is visually easy to understand what a person's demeanor is. So, yes you can, by definition, say the use of the word nose is symbolic for anger, but it is not like a slang word or a colloquialism, or a word which has a hidden meaning. The same holds true for the Hebrew usage of the word tree or trees as we see in the verses below.

NIV Da 4:19 Then Daniel (also called Belteshazzar) was greatly perplexed for a time, and his thoughts terrified him. So the king said, "Belteshazzar, do not let the dream or its meaning alarm you."
Belteshazzar answered, "My lord, if only the dream applied to your enemies and its meaning to your adversaries!
NIV Da 4:20 The tree you saw, which grew large and strong, with its top touching the sky, visible to the whole earth,
NIV Da 4:21 with beautiful leaves and abundant fruit, providing food for all, giving shelter to the beasts of the field, and having nesting places in its branches for the birds of the air—
NIV Da 4:22 __you, O king, are that tree__! You have become great and strong; your greatness has grown until it reaches the sky, and your dominion extends to distant parts of the earth.
NIV Da 4:23 "You, O king, saw a messenger, a holy one, coming down from heaven and saying, 'Cut down the tree and destroy it, but leave the stump, bound with iron and bronze, in the grass of the field, while its roots remain in the ground. Let him be drenched with the dew of heaven; let him live like the wild animals, until seven times pass by for him.'
NIV Da 4:24 "This is the interpretation, O king, and this is the decree the Most High has issued against my lord the king:
NIV Da 4:25 You will be driven away from people and will live with the wild animals; you will eat grass like cattle and be drenched with the dew of heaven. Seven times will pass by for you until you acknowledge that the Most High is sovereign over the kingdoms of men and gives them to anyone he wishes.
NIV Da 4:26 The command to leave the stump of the tree with its roots means that your kingdom will be restored to you when you acknowledge that Heaven rules.
NIV Da 4:27 Therefore, O king, be pleased to accept my advice: Renounce your sins by doing what is right, and your wickedness by being kind to the oppressed. It may be that then your prosperity will continue."

In the center of the garden there were two trees. One was the tree of life, and the other was the tree of the fruit of the knowledge of good and evil (subjective knowledge and reasoning). One tree was the Lord (the word of God) and the other was the Devil, respectively. After eating the fruit of the tree of the knowledge of good and evil, Adam and Eve and their children were denied access to the tree of life (the Lord) or to eat (ingest) its fruit (His Spirit). It was because they had chosen to pick one spirit source and its wisdom (fruit) over the other, which is antagonistic towards the Spirit and its wisdom of the tree of life.

Note: What the authors mean by the term, "subjective knowledge and subjective reasoning" when it comes to Adam and Eve is that the fruit of the knowledge of good and evil are the faculties to know both right and wrong and the faculties to judge—to have a personal opinion whether something is either good or bad (for oneself). In other words, to be aware of the fact that there is an alternative to doing what is morally right or good. To possess a cognizant contrast between the two, good and evil. Then realizing that you can judge or decide for yourself which response, the morally right and submissive, or the evil and rebellious/defiant response which suits your own perceived needs.

Before spiritually ingesting the fruit of the knowledge of good and evil, Adam and Eve were naive and did not possess that ability. Before the fall if the Lord left a loaded gun on a table in the room (as an example), then while walking out of the room told them not to touch the gun, it would not be a careless thing to do. The Lord said not to touch, so Adam and Eve not knowing there was an alternative (not possessing subjective knowledge) would never consider touching it or question why they should not (subjective reasoning). They simply would not touch it or wonder why; it would not occur to them there were options outside of God's command.

Ever since the death of Jesus and the day of Pentecost, we have access once again to the tree of life who is the Lord and His Spirit (the Holy Spirit). He told us that if we open our hearts to Him, out of us will flow rivers of living waters. That is because if we accept Him and declare Him Lord, He comes inside and cohabitates with us in our hearts—we have His Spirit. It is His Spirit that are the living waters which flow out of us because of Him cohabitating with us in our hearts (the seat of decision, and of our personality). It is a Spirit which we can perceive through from within our hearts. A Spirit which does not rely on the type of wisdom that considers through subjective knowledge and reasoning but discards it, and instead through faith, acts out of obedience to every prompting of the Lord's.

NIV 1Co 1:19 For it is written:

"I will destroy the wisdom of the wise;

the intelligence of the intelligent I will frustrate (the process of discerning and acting on subjective knowledge and reasoning, which is original sin)

NIV 1Co 1:30 It is because of him that you are in <u>Christ Jesus, who has become for us wisdom from God—that is, our righteousness</u>...

NIV Ro 8:12 <u>Therefore, brothers, we have an obligation—but it is not to the sinful nature, to live according to it.</u>
NIV Ro 8:13 For if you live according to the sinful nature (discerning and deciding through subjective knowledge and reasoning), *you will die; but if by the Spirit you put to death the misdeeds of the body, you will live,*
NIV Ro 8:14 because those who are led by the Spirit of God are sons of God

Meaning to have faith by operating out of the Lord's Spirit perspective while ignoring or overriding the ability original sin gave us to think—to discern and act out of subjective knowledge and reasoning.

NIV 1Co 2:14 The man without the Spirit does not accept the things that come from the Spirit of God, <u>for they are foolishness to him, and he cannot understand them, because they are spiritually discerned.</u>

In other words, to abandon and no longer trust what we think of as just plain common sense or as they say, "using the brain God gave us." The fact is, it is not at all the brain God gave us but the wisdom the Devil corrupted the human spirit with, in the garden, causing us to trust our own righteousness—our own ability to subjectively consider and decide from our own ideas of what is right and wrong. As it says, Christ Jesus, His Spirit in us, has become for us wisdom from God and our righteousness—our new compass which we rely on to know what is right, beneficial, and good.

However, do not let it escape us that even though we possess His Spirit within us, we can fail to have faith in what His Spirit is prompting us to do through our conscience. Then out of preference and a greater faith in our ability to think (to reason with subjective knowledge) we choose to act out of our own intelligence. His Spirit does not in these cases bear fruit in our lives, rather, we bear the fruit of our sin nature. In his book, James clarifies for us the two different wisdoms we (those who have the Spirit of God living in them) possess within us. In his description, James also helps us see and understand the different perspectives, motives, and results/fruit of both of these opposing spirit perspectives that we have, to carefully choose which to employ decision by decision.

This is a spiritual fruit of the tree of life in the spiritual city, the New Jerusalem. As we read on in Ezekiel we will see that when this river of life flows from the temple in the old Jerusalem to the Dead Sea, fruit trees of every kind line it as the tree of life does in the New Jerusalem, and they bear fruit 12 times per year, no longer yielding a single crop every 12 months.

WEB Zec 14:8 It will happen in that day, that living waters will go out from Jerusalem; half of them toward the eastern sea, and half of them toward the western sea; in summer and in winter will it be.

The River From the Temple

NIV Eze 47:1 The man (angel) *brought me back to the entrance of the temple, and I saw water coming out from under the threshold of the temple toward the east (for the temple faced east). The water was coming down from under the south side of the temple, south of the altar.*

The angel brings Ezekiel back to the entrance of the temple in the earthly Jerusalem renamed "the Lord is There" in order to show him something that is important to take note of. It is where the water from the river of life enters into the natural realm. It is also important to note that it is here that we can know for certain that Ezekiel is speaking about the millennium temple and the millennium reign of Christ on the natural earth. This is simply because the river of life is present and coming from the throne of the Lord in the supernatural city to the earthly temple.

Warning: Below is a potential case of Bible verses that contradict each other if using conventional wisdom.

John just got finished telling us that in the supernatural city, the New Jerusalem, (the home of the Lord and His Father) there is no temple; the Lord and His Father are the temple. On the other hand, Ezekiel tells us how the earthly city of Jerusalem is renamed, "JEHOVAH-SHAMMAH" (The Lord is There). In addition, Ezekiel tells us this natural city, JEHOVAH-SHAMMAH, has a temple in it. Unless you decide that either John or Ezekiel are in error, it becomes clear that they are not talking about the same place. Though they occupy the same space, Ezekiel is speaking about the natural city JEHOVAH-SHAMMAH in the revived nation of Israel, and John is talking about the supernatural city, the New Jerusalem, which somehow occupies the same space.

Likewise, John tells us that the river of life has as its source the throne of the Lord and His Father. It flows one direction from the throne down the middle of the street in the New Jerusalem while lined with the (singular) tree of life, bearing 12 different kinds fruit, 12 times a year. Ezekiel told us (above) that the angel showed him from the entrance of the temple in the city called JEHOVAH-SHAMMAH that the waters of the river of life were coming out from under the threshold of the temple and flowed to the east. He further observed that the water came down from under the south side of the temple, south of the altar. We learn below that the living waters coming out of the temple flow in two directions. One is west to the Mediterranean Sea and the other is east towards the Dead Sea. As the eastern branch moves toward the Dead Sea it is lined with all kinds of trees, in particular; "all" kinds of fruit trees which are harvested 12 times a year. Again, for comparison's sake, the same river of life in the New Jerusalem is lined with only one tree, bearing 12 different kinds of fruit, 12 times a year. However, in the natural earth, in the city JEHOVAH-SHAMMAH, the river is lined with "all kinds" of fruit trees, each bearing a crop, 12 times a year.

Additionally, in the natural realm, the river of life empties into the Dead Sea turning it into fresh water, teaming with fish. This is an event which has not yet occurred. This will only happen during the 1,000-year reign of Christ, when the New Jerusalem is present. That is because within the New Jerusalem is the source of this river of life Ezekiel is being shown. As we read on, we will see how this is true.

NIV Eze 47:2 He then brought me out through the north gate and led me around the outside to the outer gate facing east, and the water was flowing from the south side.
NIV Eze 47:3 As the man went eastward with a measuring line in his hand, he measured off a thousand cubits and then led me through water that was ankle-deep.

NIV Eze 47:4 *He measured off another thousand cubits and led me through water that was knee-deep. He measured off another thousand and led me through water that was up to the waist.* *NIV Eze 47:5* *He measured off another thousand, but now it was a river that I could not cross, because the water had risen and was deep enough to swim in—a river that no one could cross.*

The water has gone from coming down from under the south side of the temple, then coming out from under the threshold flowing east gradually turning into a river no one can ford in a little over three quarters of a mile (3,000 cubits).

NIV Eze 47:6 *He asked me, "Son of man, do you see this?" Then he led me back to the bank of the river.*
NIV Eze 47:7 *When I arrived there, I saw a great number of trees on each side of the river.*
NIV Eze 47:8 *He said to me, "This water flows toward the eastern region and goes down into the Arabah, where it enters the* (Dead) *Sea. When it empties into the Sea, the water there becomes fresh.*

Arabah is a location which defines the border between Israel and Jorden. Arabah means, "Desolate and dry area." That geographic area is now called the, "Jordan Rift Valley." After the flowing waters turn into a river, it reaches down into and across the desert valley then empties into the Dead Sea. We see in the next verse (below) that the river makes the desert come to life wherever it flows.

NIV Eze 47:9 *Swarms of living creatures will live wherever the river flows. There will be large numbers of fish, because this water flows there and makes the salt water fresh; so where the river flows everything will live.*
NIV Eze 47:10 *Fishermen will stand along the shore; from En Gedi to En Eglaim there will be places for spreading nets. The fish will be of many kinds —like the fish of the Great Sea.*

Some believe that to say from En Gedi to En Eglaim signifies that from one end to the other, along the western coast of the Dead Sea. These names may be referring to two different oases on opposite ends of the western coast. The thought is that to say; "Fishermen will stand along the shore; "from En Gedi to En Eglaim there will be places for spreading nets. The fish will be of many kinds—like the fish of the Great Sea," is the equivalent of saying from the north end to the south end, all along the western shore fishermen will line up to catch the abundant fish.

NIV Eze 47:11 But the swamps and marshes will not become fresh; they will be left for salt.
NIV Eze 47:12 Fruit trees of all kinds will grow on both banks of the river. Their leaves will not wither, nor will their fruit fail. Every month they will bear, because the water from the sanctuary flows to them. Their fruit will serve for food and their leaves for healing.

The Dead Sea has no life in it because it is saltier than the oceans by more than eight and a half times. It is nearly impossible to drown in it. You can just lay in it and float. One of the reasons it is so salty is because at 1,388 feet below sea level it is the lowest point on earth. Also, it gets very little rain fall. The only way for water to get out of the Dead Sea is for it to evaporate, causing the water to be a higher concentration of salt. The dry hot climate helps this process.

Given that, it is interesting to note that the origin of the River of Life will be from within the New Jerusalem flowing from the throne of the Lord at the top of the mountain base that the New Jerusalem sits on. There on that mountain top will be the highest point on earth we were told, and the river will empty into the Dead Sea, which is the lowest point on earth. That is given the elevation of the Dead Sea doesn't change with the shift in topography that will occur when Jesus returns and makes way for the New Jerusalem.

WEB Rev 22:3 There will be no curse any more. The throne of God and of the Lamb will be in it, and his servants serve him.

No curses. Let's take a look at that:

WEB Isa 2:3 For out of Zion the law shall go out,
and Yahweh's word from Jerusalem.
4 He will judge between the nations,
and will decide concerning many peoples;
and they shall beat their swords into plowshares,
and their spears into pruning hooks.
Nation shall not lift up sword against nation,
neither shall they learn war any more.

When Jesus was here on earth, He showed us that He had an authority above that of the Devil and the four horsemen. The four horsemen were curses put on humanity by God a couple generations after the flood. It was in answer to the rebellion of Nimrod; his tower of Babel, his city Babylon, and the whole world wanting Nimrod to be king over them to protect them from God. They crowned him king so they might do as they pleased without consequences from God (details of this are in previous volumes).

WEB Rev 6:2 And behold, a white horse, and he who sat on it had a bow. A crown was given to him, and he came out conquering, and to conquer. ³ When he opened the second seal, I heard the second living creature saying, "Come!" ⁴ Another came out, a red horse. To him who sat on it was given power to take peace from the earth, and that they should kill one another. There was given to him a great sword.

Jesus showed His authority over the curses of the four horsemen by the nature of the miracles He performed. Even authority over the last pale green horseman named, death. Every one of His miracles showed supremacy over the given authority of the curses that the four horsemen wield over the human race.

During the 1,000-year reign and because the Lord is to rule over the earth at that time, these curses of the four horsemen we currently suffer under, will not exist. War and the spirit to gather together a large army are one of those curses. As a result, there will be no manufacturing of weapons for war. What weapons which remain will be scrapped and used for other purposes. There will be no more military, and no military service, not even a national guard. Not even training for war or martial arts. How can this be? It says the Lord will settle every dispute between the nations.

Nations will not be able to rise up to dominate others and take what is not theirs. This is because they will not have the power to inspire to war or the authority to do so. Even if it was their desire to do so they would lack the spirit inspirational and charismatic power to make it happen. The power, inspiration, and charisma to stir people to war was a curse and that curse and its power in the earth ends with the beast and his false prophet, when they are thrown into the lake of fire, after the Lord fights them at Armageddon.

A visual picture of the spirit of charisma a leader might possess in order inspire large armies to fight are the verses that tell us of the frogs that come out of the mouth of the false prophet, the beast, and the Devil which seduce the people of the earth to gather together as an army to fight the Lord. Those charismatic spirits of seduction will not be present during the millennium reign, it was a curse—one of the four horsemen— and Jesus overrules that curse. What a polarized contrast! The Devil and the antichrist bring with them the four horsemen of domination, slavery, destruction, and death. That is their power to rule. Whereas the Lord brings with Him healing, individual freedom, and liberation from the four horsemen.

Here is the curse of plagues and wild beasts:

WEB Rev 6:8 And behold, a pale horse, and he who sat on it, his name was Death. Hades followed with him. Authority over one fourth of the earth, to kill with the sword, with famine, with death, and by the wild animals of the earth was given to him.

According to the World Health Organization, in today's world mosquitoes give malaria to about 200 million people and carry other diseases such as; dengue fever, yellow fever, and encephalitis. They kill an estimated 750,000 people every year. Ants kill about 300 people per year. 50,000 people die each year from snake bites. Dogs kill about 25,000 every year. The tsetse fly infects up to 30,000 people each year and an estimated 10,000 of them die. The scorpion is responsible for over 3,000 deaths per year stinging as many as 1.2 million people. Mexico alone has 1,000 deaths due to scorpions. Crocodiles and alligators kill more than a 1,000 people each year. Hippopotamus are responsible for 500 deaths per year and some estimates are as high as almost 3,000 making the hippo the most dangerous animal in Africa. Then there are deaths by lions, tigers, bears, sharks, spiders, dingo's, and a host of other wild animals.

We are told above that disease will also pass away and animals who are predators will no longer be so because that too was a curse. In the garden, the serpent walked upright and was the most beautiful animal. The serpent and man sinned against the Creator of the universe. Man lost his heavenly stature. He was cut off from the fruit of the tree of life, then doomed to eat from the grasses of the field (wheat, for example). He was very dismayed, even appalled. The Talmud says this of that occasion:

"In the Talmud it is related that when Adam heard the words of God, "Thou shalt eat the herb of the fields" (Gen. iii. 18), he trembled in his limbs, and exclaimed, "O Lord of the world! I and my beast, the ass, shall have to eat out of the same manger (trough)!" But God said to him, because he trembled, "Thou shalt eat bread in the sweat of thy brow.""[2]

The Bible tells us that when the curse of sin (the power and the authority the four horsemen have over the earth) is lifted by the power and authority of Jesus; the lion will eat grass like the lamb, and they shall lay together. As for the snake:

NIV Ge 3:14 So the LORD God said to the serpent, "Because you have done this,
"Cursed are you above all the livestock
and all the wild animals!
<u>*You will crawl on your belly*</u>
<u>*and you will eat dust*</u>
all the days of your life.

At that time, when the lion is no longer a flesh-eating predator during the reign of Christ, we are told that the snake, however, will fall to the bottom of the food chain much lower than the lion and man, but as the worm who eats the soil of the earth for its sustenance.

Note: Although this humiliation was too great to bear for Adam, it was meant to humble him; to make him ripe for redemption; to counteract the effect that the eating of the fruit of the tree of the knowledge of good and evil which deluded him into seeing himself as "like (or equal to) God."

However, let's relate this to the humiliation the Lord went through in order to bring redemption to man:

NIV Jn 6:31 Our forefathers ate the manna in the desert; as it is written: 'He gave them bread from heaven to eat.'"
NIV Jn 6:32 Jesus said to them, "I tell you the truth, it is not Moses who has given you the bread from heaven, but it is my Father who gives you the true bread from heaven.
NIV Jn 6:33 For the bread of God is he who comes down from heaven and gives life to the world."
NIV Jn 6:34 "Sir," they said, "from now on give us this bread."

NIV Jn 6:35 Then Jesus declared, "<u>I am the bread of life</u>. He who comes to me will never go hungry, and he who believes in me will never be thirsty.

NIV Jn 6:48 <u>I am the bread of life.</u>
NIV Jn 6:49 Your forefathers ate the manna in the desert, yet they died.
NIV Jn 6:50 <u>But here is the bread that comes down from heaven, which a man may eat and not die.</u>
NIV Jn 6:51 <u>I am the living bread that came down from heaven. If anyone eats of this bread, he will</u> <u>live forever. This bread is my flesh, which I will give for the life of the world."</u>
NIV Jn 6:52 Then the Jews began to argue sharply among themselves, "How can this man give us his flesh to eat?"
NIV Jn 6:53 Jesus said to them, "I tell you the truth, unless you eat the flesh of the Son of Man and drink his blood, you have no life in you.
NIV Jn 6:54 Whoever eats my flesh and drinks my blood has eternal life, and I will raise him up at the last day.
NIV Jn 6:55 <u>For my flesh is real food and my blood is real drink.</u>
NIV Jn 6:56 <u>Whoever eats my flesh and drinks my blood remains in me, and I in him.</u>
NIV Jn 6:57 <u>Just as the living Father sent me and I live because of the Father, so the one who feeds</u> <u>on me will live because of me.</u>
NIV Jn 6:58 This is the bread that came down from heaven. Your forefathers ate manna and died, but he who feeds on this bread will live forever."
NIV Jn 6:59 He said this while teaching in the synagogue in Capernaum.

NIV Lk 2:4 So Joseph also went up from the town of Nazareth in Galilee to Judea, to Bethlehem the town of David, because he belonged to the house and line of David.
NIV Lk 2:5 He went there to register with Mary, who was pledged to be married to him and was expecting a child.
NIV Lk 2:6 While they were there, the time came for the baby to be born,
NIV Lk 2:7 and <u>she gave birth to her firstborn, a son. She wrapped him in cloths and placed him</u> <u>in a manger,</u> because there was no room for them in the inn.

It is very interesting that Jesus claimed that He is the bread of life, considering He was born in a town called Bethlehem; which translated means, "the house of bread." Then, upon His birth, He was placed in a manger (trough). The trough which the ass feeds out of—that which Adam was humiliated to eat the contents of—grasses/wheat (bread). Jesus is the tree of life but once we were cut off from Him—to ingest the fruit of His life-giving Spirit in the Garden. However, He has at long last come back to give to those who would believe the bread of life. By being humble and eating of this bread that came down from heaven, the Lord can give us eternal life as we once received from Him as the tree of life. He can once again be for us, our righteousness, and our wisdom from heaven; replacing the dependency on the wisdom of subjective reasoning with the perspective of doing one's own will.

When it comes to man who was seduced and now suffers death, it is by being humbled in his stature that he actually can find his redemption. He will, in his humility, be free from the death that plagues him. As for the one who seduced, the serpent/snake who lost his arms and legs and now slithers on its belly, but still for a while remains proud, deadly, and at the top of the food chain still causing death: As sentenced by the Lord will in the end, when man gains back the gift of life, become the lowest of the low and eat the soil which contains the decaying life of plants, animals, and humans including their waste, as does the worm. He will eat of the death he brought into the world.

Isaiah continues below.

WEB Isa 65:20 *"No more will there be an infant who only lives a few days,*
nor an old man who has not filled his days;
for the child will die one hundred years old,
and the sinner being one hundred years old will be accursed.

It is here in the verse above that we see mortal humans will continue to die during the 1,000-year reign of Christ. War will no longer rob humanity of their young. The mortality rate will decrease if not eradicated. Life expectancy will soar significantly higher than we know it now. Disease will no longer bring people to an early grave. However, death is still the end of mortal humans.

WEB Isa 65:21 *They will build houses, and inhabit them.*
They will plant vineyards, and eat their fruit.
22 They will not build, and another inhabit.
They will not plant, and another eat:
for the days of my people will be like the days of a tree,
and my chosen will long enjoy the work of their hands.

²³ They will not labor in vain,
nor give birth for calamity;
for they are the offspring of Yahweh's blessed,
and their descendants with them.
²⁴ It will happen that, before they call, I will answer;
and while they are yet speaking, I will hear.
²⁵ The wolf and the lamb will feed together,
and the lion will eat straw like the ox.
Dust will be the serpent's food.
They will not hurt nor destroy in all my holy mountain,"
says Yahweh.

The curse of not being able to communicate because of language barriers will end. Below we are told how the different languages began:

WEB Ge 11:5 Yahweh came down to see the city and the tower, which the children of men built. ⁶ Yahweh said, "Behold, they are one people, and they have all one language, and this is what they begin to do. Now nothing will be withheld from them, which they intend to do. ⁷ Come, let's go down, and there confuse their language, that they may not understand one another's speech." ⁸ So Yahweh scattered them abroad from there on the surface of all the earth. They stopped building the city. ⁹ Therefore its name was called Babel, because there Yahweh confused the language of all the earth. From there, Yahweh scattered them abroad on the surface of all the earth.

Here we see in Zephaniah this curse too will be eliminated:

Amp Zep 3:9 For then [changing their impure language] I will give to the people a clear and pure speech from pure lips, that they may all call upon the name of the Lord, to serve Him with one unanimous consent and one united shoulder [bearing the yoke of the Lord].

After this, we are told the nation of Israel will surround "the city," giving room for all twelve tribes. We are also told how the new Israel is to be divided up among the 12 tribes and a millennium temple will be in it. Many want to believe that the nation of Israel which exists today is the fulfillment of this promise. Although it may be a partial fulfillment, this is not the case. In spite of the fact that the nation is currently called Israel, it really is primarily a nation of the Jews, the tribes of Judah and Benjamin. For the millennium promise to be fulfilled there must be 12 states with representation of all 12 tribes in the nation. However, the Jews, their occupation of Jerusalem, and the temple (not yet built) are all important for the stage to be set for the end times to begin. For this to happen, it will be a feat only God could accomplish.

We will go back to the narrative of Ezekiel who gives us details of how life will be during the millennium reign of Jesus in the preceding chapter.

Notes

[2] Baring-Gould, S. (1871) Legends of Old Testament Characters, from the Talmud and other sources. London: R. Clay, Sons, and Taylor, Printers.

CHAPTER 4

The New Temple Area

E zekiel is taken in the spirit in a vision to see the temple of the Lord in Israel in the millennium reign. He is given instruction and shown measurements and told to pay close attention, so he could report it to Israel. The Lord shows him all this to tell the people during their exile in Babylon. At this time, it has been 25 years since the temple and city were destroyed, marking the beginning of the mass exile. Surely the Lord intended to give His people hope and a future when there was no hope by releasing this message. By passing this word of the Lord's to the people, Ezekiel was true to the meaning of his name, "God strengthens."

NIV Eze 40:1 In the twenty-fifth year of our exile, at the beginning of the year, on the tenth of the month, in the fourteenth year after the fall of the city —on that very day the hand of the LORD was upon me and he took me there.
NIV Eze 40:2 In visions of God he took me to the land of Israel and set me on a very high mountain, on whose south side were some buildings that looked like a city.
NIV Eze 40:3 He took me there, and I saw a man whose appearance was like bronze; he was standing in the gateway with a linen cord and a measuring rod in his hand.
NIV Eze 40:4 The man said to me, "Son of man, look with your eyes and hear with your ears and pay attention to everything I am going to show you, for that is why you have been brought here. Tell the house of Israel everything you see."

Then, he is shown the whole temple area. First, he is shown the wall all around the temple area, then the east gate which leads into the outer court. He moves from there to the inner court to the rooms used for the priests and the one used for preparing the sacrifices.

From there he is brought through the temple itself. Along the way he is shown how it is decorated and given measurements for its construction. After climbing the stairs of the temple and seeing its pillars, he is told by the angel where the outer sanctuary and inner sanctuary (the Most Holy Place) is to be.

Ezekiel is then taken back out to the outer court and to the rooms made for the priest. He is told:

NIV Eze 42:13 Then he said to me, "The north and south rooms facing the temple courtyard are the priests' rooms, <u>where the priests who approach the LORD will eat the most holy offerings. There they will put the most holy offerings—the grain offerings, the sin offerings and the guilt offerings—for the place is holy.</u>
NIV Eze 42:14 Once the priests enter the holy precincts, they are not to go into the outer court until they leave behind the garments in which they minister, for these are holy. They are to put on other clothes before they go near the places that are for the people.

The Glory Returns to the Temple

NIV Eze 43:1 Then the man (the angel) *brought me to the gate facing east,*
NIV Eze 43:2 and I saw the glory of the God of Israel coming from the east. His voice was like the roar of rushing waters, and the land was radiant with his glory.
NIV Eze 43:3 The vision I saw was like the vision I had seen when he came to destroy the city (Jerusalem) *and like the visions I had seen by the Kebar River, and I fell facedown.*

The first thing to take note of, which is important, is that Ezekiel sees the "glory" of the Lord return to the temple. Not the Lord, but His glory, and His voice. Somewhere within all the radiated glory which shines like the sun, illuminating the earth while coming towards the temple is the source, the Lord and God of Israel. The setting for this time period is the millennium reign when Christ is on the earth for 1,000-years cohabitating with mortal men and ruler of the entire world.

The significance of this we will see as we read on. However, we must keep in mind that unlike John who sees this time period (described in Revelation) from a celestial perspective, as a celestial human, Ezekiel sees his vision from the natural perspective as a natural or mortal human. John sees the Lord come to Jerusalem in His Spiritual body and tells us that we who become celestial beings will fellowship/talk with Him face-to-face in the New Jerusalem. John sees celestial humans before the throne of the Lord with its heavenly Sanhedrin. Furthermore, there is no temple, but Jesus and His Father are the temple in the spiritual city, the New Jerusalem.

Conversely, Ezekiel sees from the perspective of a natural human, the natural counterpart to the celestial city, the New Jerusalem—the earthly city JEHOVAH-SHAMMAH (The Lord is There). From a natural human perspective, Ezekiel sees (instead of the Lord's form face-to-face) the glory of the Lord—the splendor of His Spirit which illuminates an earth that has been plunged into utter darkness. He sees the Lord's glory coming from the east to the west and into the temple of that natural city, to fellowship with natural humans who are represented by the prince of the newly formed Israel and by the priests of the temple.

This is the extent that a mortal human can take in of the Lord, not being able to see past the illumination of His glory; in order to see His true form. Only in a vision, which is merely a representative manifestation, can a human see a visible image of the Lord. It is said that if a mortal human sees the Lord, he will die.

NRSV Ex 33:18 Moses said, "Show me your glory, I pray." 19 And he said, "I will make all my goodness pass before you, and will proclaim before you the name, 'The LORD'; and I will be gracious to whom I will be gracious, and will show mercy on whom I will show mercy. 20 But," he said, "you cannot see my face; for no one shall see me and live." 21 And the LORD continued, "See, there is a place by me where you shall stand on the rock; 22 and while my glory passes by I will put you in a cleft of the rock, and I will cover you with my hand until I have passed by; 23 then I will take away my hand, and you shall see my back; but my face shall not be seen."

Below, the Lord passes by Elijah showing him His back as well:

NRSV 1Ki 19:11 *He said, "Go out and stand on the mountain before the LORD, for the LORD is about to pass by." Now there was a great wind, so strong that it was splitting mountains and breaking rocks in pieces before the LORD, but the LORD was not in the wind; and after the wind an earthquake, but the LORD was not in the earthquake; ¹² and after the earthquake a fire, but the LORD was not in the fire; and after the fire a sound of sheer silence. ¹³ When Elijah heard it, he wrapped his face in his mantle and went out and stood at the entrance of the cave. Then there came a voice to him that said, "What are you doing here, Elijah?"*

As intense as this is, seeing the glory of the Lord coming to the temple, Ezekiel says it was the same when he saw the Lord come to Jerusalem before the Babylonian Armies of Nebuchadnezzar to destroy it. How horrible it must have been to be able to have a sense of and see the Lord's glory and anger sweep over the land, leading the armies who all but completely destroy your whole civilization, carting off those who are left. We are referring to the Lord who loved you, and gave you everything, including your civilization. How terrible it must have felt to have reaped the wrath of the invisible but loving and merciful God, who warned you time after time of your ways.

Sometimes we mess with fire and we are oblivious to what we are calling down on ourselves. However, it is an oblivion we bring upon ourselves. How and why? In our determination to do our own will, and indulge our own desires, we put out of our minds that the Lord is not only real but is a person in the sense that He is not an object. He has feelings and is moved by our interaction with Him. He can get offended, be shown disloyalty, be and feel betrayed, jealous, taken advantage of and objectified. He has a dignity and is owed a reverence and respect as a living being. He is the source of all life! However, when we lose Him as our first love and instead love ourselves, serving Him becomes something to contend with as we give our focus over to serving ourselves. Since He is invisible and for the time being we (in general, as mortal humans) can only have a sense of His Spirit within us; it is easy to forget all those things, and just betray Him like a husband who brings home his lovers in full view of his wife, not believing she will do anything about it, or have the right to be hurt over it.

Joel too describes God's glory sweeping across the land before an army, which the Lord used in His anger to discipline Israel. In Joel's case, it was the Assyrian Army. Ezekiel had brought to mind the same exact experience of the Lord's glory sweeping over the land in anger which came before the Babylonian Army. In Joel's case we can have a more detailed picture of what that looks like.

WEB Joel 2:1 *Blow the trumpet in Zion,*
and sound an alarm in my holy mountain!
Let all the inhabitants of the land tremble,
for the day of Yahweh comes,
for it is close at hand:
² A day of darkness and gloominess,
a day of clouds and thick darkness.
As the dawn spreading on the mountains (the light of God coming from the east to the west and a rising sun),
a great and strong people;
there has never been the like,
neither will there be any more after them,
even to the years of many generations.
³ A fire devours before them,
and behind them, a flame burns.
The land is as the garden of Eden before them,
and behind them, a desolate wilderness.
Yes, and no one has escaped them.
⁴ Their appearance is as the appearance of horses,
and as horsemen, so do they run.
⁵ Like the noise of chariots on the tops of the mountains do they leap,
like the noise of a flame of fire that devours the stubble,
as a strong people set in battle array.
⁶ At their presence the peoples are in anguish.
All faces have grown pale.
⁷ They run like mighty men (like giants).
They climb the wall like warriors.
They each march in his line, and they don't swerve off course.
⁸ Neither does one jostle another;
they march everyone in his path,
and they burst through the defenses,

and don't break ranks.
⁹ They rush on the city.
They run on the wall.
They climb up into the houses.
They enter in at the windows like thieves.
¹⁰ The earth quakes before them.
The heavens tremble.
The sun and the moon are darkened,
and the stars withdraw their shining.
¹¹ Yahweh thunders his voice before his army;
for his forces are very great;
for he (the invading army) *is strong who obeys his command;*
for the day of Yahweh is great and very awesome,
and who can endure it?

The Christians made these words a song. Many sing and dance to it completely ignorant that this prophetic oracle was the Lord coming against His own people and leading or marching out before their enemies to destroy them. They mistakenly see themselves as the army behind His glory, overwhelming and conquering the city. They see it as a banner of victory over their enemies. In reality, the city Joel speaks of are the cities of Israel! It is the Lord's people who are melting with fear and are being overrun, their garden of Eden going up in flames leaving behind nothing but ashes.

It is the same for us concerning what John speaks to us as it was for what Joel spoke to his nation, Israel. Joel warned them, and they did not listen. John tells us in Revelation about the coming great tribulation that will befall the *Church Corrupt*:

The Voice Rev17:16 The beast and the ten horns you saw will despise the whore; they will make her a wasteland and strip her naked. They will gorge themselves on her flesh and incinerate her with fire. ¹⁷ For God has placed in their hearts to do what He has purposed, that is, to become one in mind and to surrender their kingdoms over to the beast until the words of God accomplish their end.

This sounds so absurd to us, even so much so to the translators that they find it hard (in most translations) to interpret this as it says, that God is "to become one in mind" with the beast and the ten kings. Nevertheless, these verses tell us that God "placed" it into their (the beast and the ten kings) hearts to hate the *Church Corrupt* and destroy her. And that He, God, becomes "one in mind" with them (the beast and the ten kings) to utterly destroy the Church in the earth. God is in agreement, He is taking up the same cause to hate the Church and destroy it.

NIV Rev 18:8 *Therefore in one day her plagues will overtake her:*
death, mourning and famine.
She will be consumed by fire,
for mighty is the Lord God who judges her.

Finally, God "surrenders" the Church and its kingdoms (domains) over to the beast and the 10 kings as He did to Israel with both the Assyrians, and later with the Babylonians. They too (as us) would not accept that God would pay them back for their sins. They did not believe God would ever give Jerusalem over to their enemies. For John predicts the Church will say the same in her heart as they did:

NIV Rev 18:7 *Give her as much torture and grief*
as the glory and luxury she gave herself.
In her heart she boasts,
'I sit as queen; I am not a widow,
and I will never mourn.'

Our consolation is this: The *Church Pure* will be raptured the day the great tribulation will overtake the *Church Corrupt*. In addition, those who endure His wrath, staying true to their profession of faith, even to death, will become celestial humans at the first resurrection and rule with Christ over the mortal humans upon His return.

Once, many years ago in the distant past, I engaged in an activity that was a sin. At the prospect of my wife finding out, I prayed feverantly asking the Lord to not let her find out. I was so petrified that she might. If she had, I had no idea how she would react. I could only imagine the degree it would make her angry, hurt, and maybe lose her trust in me. At the thought of that I could see it might take a long time for her to regain trust in me. I just could not bear the consequences if she was to find out. So, I tearfully begged the Lord in prayer to help.

Then, in my franticness, the Lord spoke to me saying, what about Me? Because I am invisible you have no fear of me? You know well that I see all things and you sinned right before Me, however, you are only concerned with how your wife, who is visible, may feel? You are not concerned whatsoever with how it provokes my anger, and divides you from Me, because you have been unfaithful to Me who is not visible? Then you come to Me as if it has no effect on our relationship and as if I am your partner in crime, asking Me to help you keep this from being exposed? Because I am unseen, you have no fear and objectify me as if it does not affect Me, and you worry not how it provokes me to anger against you.

As Abraham was quoted as saying often, "He who is not seen, sees all."

It's time to take the warnings of the Lord, who is the Spirit of prophecy from God, seriously:

WEB Mt 23:29 "Woe to you, scribes and Pharisees, hypocrites! For you build the tombs of the prophets, and decorate the tombs of the righteous, 30 and say, 'If we had lived in the days of our fathers, we wouldn't have been partakers with them in the blood of the prophets.' 31 Therefore you testify to yourselves that you are children of those who killed the prophets. 32 Fill up, then, the measure of your fathers. 33 You serpents, you offspring of vipers, how will you escape the judgment of Gehenna? 34 Therefore behold, I send to you prophets, wise men, and scribes. Some of them you will kill and crucify; and some of them you will scourge in your synagogues, and persecute from city to city; 35 that on you may come all the righteous blood shed on the earth, from the blood of righteous Abel to the blood of Zachariah son of Barachiah, whom you killed between the sanctuary and the altar. 36 Most certainly I tell you, all these things will come upon this generation. 37 "Jerusalem, Jerusalem, who kills the prophets, and stones those who are sent to her! How often I would have gathered your children together, even as a hen gathers her chicks under her wings, and you would not (were not willing)! 38 Behold, your house is left to you desolate. 39 For I tell you, you will not see me from now on, until you say, 'Blessed is he who comes in the name of the Lord!'"

The time of the end is at the doorstep! It is 11:59! The Lord has told us! Can we, as His people, just once, wake up from our slumber? Can we once heed the warning of Him who is unseen? Can we see what is really important? Can we be more concerned with what is invisible and is to come, instead of what is visible, and what we want in the moment? Even the squirrels gather nuts for the winter. Will we have to suffer that which is unendurable just as the Lord's people have in all of history? Will we be broken, unable to endure another moment, waiting for the day of His return, saying: "Blessed is he who comes in the name of the Lord"? All because the only thing real to us is what will serve ourselves? The invisible must become more real if we are to avoid the coming judgment. Only time will tell who took into his heart this message of the Lord's (Revelation) He gave to His people, His elect.

Returning back to the vision of Ezekiel seeing the glory of the Lord, returning to His people after all His wrath had been poured out.

NIV Eze 43:4 The glory of the LORD entered the temple through the gate facing east.

NIV Eze 43:5 Then the Spirit lifted me up and brought me into the inner court, and the glory of the LORD filled the temple.

NIV Eze 43:6 While the man was standing beside me, I heard someone speaking to me from inside the temple.

NIV Eze 43:7 He said: "Son of man, this is the place of my throne and the place for the soles of my feet. This is where I will live among the Israelites forever. The house of Israel will never again defile my holy name—neither they nor their kings—by their prostitution and the lifeless idols of their kings at their high places.

NIV Eze 43:8 When they placed their threshold next to my threshold and their doorposts beside my doorposts, with only a wall between me and them, they defiled my holy name by their detestable practices. So I destroyed them in my anger.

NIV Eze 43:9 Now let them put away from me their prostitution and the lifeless idols of their kings, and I will live among them forever.

NIV Eze 43:10 "Son of man, describe the temple to the people of Israel, that they may be ashamed of their sins. Let them consider the plan,

NIV Eze 43:11 and if they are ashamed of all they have done, make known to them the design of the temple—its arrangement, its exits and entrances—its whole design and all its regulations and laws. Write these down before them so that they may be faithful to its design and follow all its regulations.

NIV Eze 43:12 "This is the law of the temple: All the surrounding area on top of the mountain will be most holy. Such is the law of the temple.

It is the Lord who speaks to Ezekiel and not the angel. He shows Ezekiel the altar, its regulations, and what should be sacrificed for what occasion. The angel resumes, bringing Ezekiel through the rest of what the Lord wants him to see and report. The Lord says to Ezekiel, "Son of man, this is the place of my throne and the place for the soles of my feet. This is where I will live among the Israelites forever." The Lord said through Isaiah:

NIV Isa 66:1 This is what the LORD says:
"Heaven is my throne,
and the earth is my footstool.

These words are in line with the 1,000-year reign of Christ, that is, when the earth moves into the spiritual or heavenly realm. The Lord's residence and throne is in the New Jerusalem, a celestial city made of celestial matter. However, the celestial city which the seat of His throne occupies, rests upon the earth where the soles of His feet touch.

The Prince, the Levites, the Priests

NIV Eze 44:1 Then the man brought me back to the outer gate of the sanctuary, the one facing east, and it was shut.
NIV Eze 44:2 The LORD said to me, "This gate is to remain shut. It must not be opened; no one may enter through it. It is to remain shut because the LORD, the God of Israel, has entered through it.
NIV Eze 44:3 The prince himself is the only one who may sit inside the gateway to eat in the presence of the LORD. He is to enter by way of the portico of the gateway and go out the same way."

The prince the Lord is referring to, is the mortal leader of the nation of Israel during the millennium reign of Christ. In addition to him, each tribe will have a prince over them who is subject to this prince over all of Israel.

NIV Eze 44:4 Then the man brought me by way of the north gate to the front of the temple. I looked and saw the glory of the LORD filling the temple of the LORD, and I fell facedown.

NIV Eze 44:5 The LORD said to me, "Son of man, look carefully, listen closely and give attention to everything I tell you concerning all the regulations regarding the temple of the LORD. Give attention to the entrance of the temple and all the exits of the sanctuary.

NIV Eze 44:6 Say to the rebellious house of Israel, 'This is what the Sovereign LORD says: Enough of your detestable practices, O house of Israel!

NIV Eze 44:7 In addition to all your other detestable practices, you brought foreigners uncircumcised in heart and flesh into my sanctuary, desecrating my temple while you offered me food, fat and blood, and you broke my covenant.

NIV Eze 44:8 Instead of carrying out your duty in regard to my holy things, you put others in charge of my sanctuary.

NIV Eze 44:9 This is what the Sovereign LORD says: No foreigner uncircumcised in heart and flesh is to enter my sanctuary, not even the foreigners who live among the Israelites.

NIV Eze 44:10 " 'The Levites who went far from me when Israel went astray and who wandered from me after their idols must bear the consequences of their sin.

NIV Eze 44:11 They may serve in my sanctuary, having charge of the gates of the temple and serving in it; they may slaughter the burnt offerings and sacrifices for the people and stand before the people and serve them.

NIV Eze 44:12 But because they served them in the presence of their idols and made the house of Israel fall into sin, therefore I have sworn with uplifted hand that they must bear the consequences of their sin, declares the Sovereign LORD.

NIV Eze 44:13 They are not to come near to serve me as priests or come near any of my holy things or my most holy offerings; they must bear the shame of their detestable practices.

NIV Eze 44:14 Yet I will put them in charge of the duties of the temple and all the work that is to be done in it.

NIV Eze 44:15 " 'But the priests, who are Levites and descendants of Zadok and who faithfully carried out the duties of my sanctuary when the Israelites went astray from me, are to come near to minister before me; they are to stand before me to offer sacrifices of fat and blood, declares the Sovereign LORD.

NIV Eze 44:16 They alone are to enter my sanctuary; they alone are to come near my table to minister before me and perform my service.

NIV Eze 44:17 " 'When they enter the gates of the inner court, they are to wear linen clothes; they must not wear any woolen garment while ministering at the gates of the inner court or inside the temple.

NIV Eze 44:18 They are to wear linen turbans on their heads and linen undergarments around their waists. They must not wear anything that makes them perspire.

NIV Eze 44:19 When they go out into the outer court where the people are, they are to take off the clothes they have been ministering in and are to leave them in the sacred rooms, and put on other clothes, so that they do not consecrate the people by means of their garments.

The presence of the Lord's Spirit will be so overpowering that in just serving the sacrifices in the earthly temple, where the presence of the Lord comes, the garments of the priests will be so radiant with the life giving Spirit of the Lord's that they can impart the power of God. In the days of temple worship when the presence of the Lord would come to the Holy of Holies if the high priest was not properly sanctified or did not do something as properly prescribed, he would die. The presence of God was so powerful and so pure in the Holy of Holies that if anyone entered in who was not sanctified or had sin, he would die.

Conversely, the following 2 verses tell us of the power in the garments of Jesus and Paul:

NIV Mk 5:27 When she heard about Jesus, she came up behind him in the crowd and touched his cloak,

NIV Mk 5:28 because she thought, "If I just touch his clothes, I will be healed."

NIV Mk 5:29 Immediately her bleeding stopped and she felt in her body that she was freed from her suffering.

NIV Mk 5:30 At once Jesus realized that power had gone out from him. He turned around in the crowd and asked, "Who touched my clothes?"

NIV Ac 19:11 God did extraordinary miracles through Paul,

NIV Ac 19:12 so that even handkerchiefs and aprons that had touched him were taken to the sick, and their illnesses were cured and the evil spirits left them.

As stated above, in the case of the high priest entering into the Holy of Holies before Christ, they would die if they were not pure and properly sanctified. However, after Christ released His Spirit in the earth through His death, if anyone is as little as being exposed to the garments of those possessing the Holy Spirit, they would become healed and delivered from whatever evil spirit they were in bondage to.

During the millennium reign and when the Lord is living on the earth in the New Jerusalem, if the priest ministers the sacrifice to the Lord when His presence is in the earthly temple, and if he were to wear the same clothes among the people; the presence or Spirit of the Lord will be so strong on those consecrated garments that it will consecrate the people as sacred and set apart— creatures for the purposes of being present before the Lord. This is as close to the edge as it gets for a mortal human, short of being before His throne in the New Jerusalem, clothed in a celestial body.

NIV Rev 21:25 On no day will its gates ever be shut, for there will be no night there.

NIV Rev 21:26 The glory and honor of the nations will be brought into it.

NIV Rev 21:27 Nothing impure will ever enter it, nor will anyone who does what is shameful or deceitful, but only those whose names are written in the Lamb's book of life.

NIV Rev 22:3 . . . The throne of God and of the Lamb will be in the (celestial) *city* (the New Jerusalem), *and his* servants (the celestial humans who came down from Heaven with the Lord) *will serve him.*

NIV Rev 22:4 They will see his face, and his name will be on their foreheads.

This is a role that only the celestial humans that come down to the earth with the Lord can fulfill. For it says that nothing unclean (such as a mortal body) can enter the New Jerusalem, likewise, that it is the celestial humans with the Lord in the New Jerusalem who will see Him face-to-face, talk to Him and receive their daily missions from Him before His throne.

Below, Ezekiel continues to prophesy about the temple in "the city" of the natural world, during the reign of Christ. He explains the requirements for the mortal human priests who serve in it.

NIV Eze 44:20 " 'They must not shave their heads or let their hair grow long, but they are to keep the hair of their heads trimmed.

NIV Eze 44:21 No priest is to drink wine when he enters the inner court.

NIV Eze 44:22 They must not marry widows or divorced women; they may marry only virgins of Israelite descent or widows of priests.

NIV Eze 44:23 They are to teach my people the difference between the holy and the common and show them how to distinguish between the unclean and the clean.

NIV Eze 44:24 " 'In any dispute, the priests are to serve as judges and decide it according to my ordinances. They are to keep my laws and my decrees for all my appointed feasts and they are to keep my Sabbaths holy.

NIV Eze 44:25 " 'A priest must not defile himself by going near a dead person; however, if the dead person was his father or mother, son or daughter, brother or unmarried sister, then he may defile himself.

NIV Eze 44:26 After he is cleansed, he must wait seven days.

NIV Eze 44:27 On the day he goes into the inner court of the sanctuary to minister in the sanctuary, he is to offer a sin offering for himself, declares the Sovereign LORD.

NIV Eze 44:28 " 'I am to be the only inheritance the priests have. You are to give them no possession in Israel; I will be their possession.

NIV Eze 44:29 They will eat the grain offerings, the sin offerings and the guilt offerings; and everything in Israel devoted to the LORD will belong to them.

NIV Eze 44:30 The best of all the firstfruits and of all your special gifts will belong to the priests. You are to give them the first portion of your ground meal so that a blessing may rest on your household.

NIV Eze 44:31 The priests must not eat anything, bird or animal, found dead or torn by wild animals.

Next, Ezekiel is brought through the division of the land for both the holy purposes and the municipal purposes. This includes how part of the land is to be set aside for the "sacred district", where the temple will be. As well, where the Levites will live and the area which is called, "the city" where the Lord's prince of Israel will rule from. It goes on with how the nation of Israel is to be divided up among the twelve tribes. Ezekiel is then given instructions on offerings and holy days.

Offerings and Holy Days

NIV Eze 45:13 " 'This is the special gift you are to offer: a sixth of an ephah from each homer of wheat and a sixth of an ephah from each homer of barley.

NIV Eze 45:14 The prescribed portion of oil, measured by the bath, is a tenth of a bath from each cor (which consists of ten baths or one homer, for ten baths are equivalent to a homer).

NIV Eze 45:15 Also one sheep is to be taken from every flock of two hundred from the well-watered pastures of Israel. These will be used for the grain offerings, burnt offerings and fellowship offerings to make atonement for the people, declares the Sovereign LORD.

NIV Eze 45:16 All the people of the land will participate in this special gift for the use of the prince in Israel.

NIV Eze 45:17 It will be the duty of the prince to provide the burnt offerings, grain offerings and drink offerings at the festivals, the New Moons and the Sabbaths —at all the appointed feasts of the house of Israel. He will provide the sin offerings, grain offerings, burnt offerings and fellowship offerings to make atonement for the house of Israel.

NIV Eze 45:18 " 'This is what the Sovereign LORD says: <u>In the first month on the first day</u> (this would be like a new year's celebration) *you are to take a young bull without defect and purify the sanctuary.*

NIV Eze 45:19 The priest is to take some of the blood of the sin offering and put it on the doorposts of the temple, on the four corners of the upper ledge of the altar and on the gateposts of the inner court.

NIV Eze 45:20 You are to do the same on the seventh day of the month for anyone who sins unintentionally or through ignorance; so you are to make atonement for the temple.

NIV Eze 45:21 " '<u>In the first month on the fourteenth day you are to observe the Passover, a feast lasting seven days</u>, during which you shall eat bread made without yeast.

NIV Eze 45:22 On that day the prince is to provide a bull as a sin offering for himself and for all the people of the land.

NIV Eze 45:23 Every day during the seven days of the Feast he is to provide seven bulls and seven rams without defect as a burnt offering to the LORD, and a male goat for a sin offering.

NIV Eze 45:24 He is to provide as a grain offering an ephah for each bull and an ephah for each ram, along with a hin of oil for each ephah.

NIV Eze 45:25 " 'During the seven days of the Feast, which begins in the seventh month on the fifteenth day, he is to make the same provision for sin offerings, burnt offerings, grain offerings and oil.

NIV Eze 46:1 " 'This is what the Sovereign LORD says: The gate of the inner court facing east is to be shut on the six working days, but on the Sabbath day and on the day of the New Moon it is to be opened.

NIV Eze 46:2 The prince is to enter from the outside through the portico of the gateway and stand by the gatepost. The priests are to sacrifice his burnt offering and his fellowship offerings. He *is to worship at the threshold of the gateway and then go out, but the gate will not be shut until evening.*

NIV Eze 46:3 <u>On the Sabbaths and New Moons the people of the land are to worship in the presence of the LORD at the entrance to that gateway.</u>

NIV Eze 46:4 The burnt offering the prince brings to the LORD on the Sabbath day is to be six male lambs and a ram, all without defect.

NIV Eze 46:5 The grain offering given with the ram is to be an ephah, and the grain offering with the lambs is to be as much as he pleases, along with a hin of oil for each ephah.

NIV Eze 46:6 On the day of the New Moon he is to offer a young bull, six lambs and a ram, all without defect.

NIV Eze 46:7 He is to provide as a grain offering one ephah with the bull, one ephah with the ram, and with the lambs as much as he wants to give, along with a hin of oil with each ephah.

NIV Eze 46:8 When the prince enters, he is to go in through the portico of the gateway, and he is to come out the same way.

NIV Eze 46:9 " 'When the people of the land come before the LORD at the appointed feasts, whoever enters by the north gate to worship is to go out the south gate; and whoever enters by the south gate is to go out the north gate. No one is to return through the gate by which he entered, but each is to go out the opposite gate.

NIV Eze 46:10 The prince is to be among them, going in when they go in and going out when they go out.

NIV Eze 46:11 " 'At the festivals and the appointed feasts, the grain offering is to be an ephah with a bull, an ephah with a ram, and with the lambs as much as one pleases, along with a hin of oil for each ephah.

NIV Eze 46:12 When the prince provides a freewill offering to the LORD—whether a burnt offering or fellowship offerings—the gate facing east is to be opened for him. He shall offer his burnt offering or his fellowship offerings as he does on the Sabbath day. Then he shall go out, and after he has gone out, the gate will be shut.

NIV Eze 46:13 " <u>Every day you are to provide a year-old lamb without defect for a burnt offering to the LORD; morning by morning you shall provide it.</u>

NIV Eze 46:14 You are also to provide with it morning by morning a grain offering, consisting of a sixth of an ephah with a third of a hin of oil to moisten the flour. The presenting of this grain offering to the LORD is a lasting ordinance.

NIV Eze 46:15 So the lamb and the grain offering and the oil shall be provided morning by morning for a regular burnt offering.

NIV Eze 46:16 " *'This is what the Sovereign LORD says: If the prince makes a gift from his inheritance to one of his sons, it will also belong to his descendants; it is to be their property by inheritance.*

NIV Eze 46:17 If, however, he makes a gift from his inheritance to one of his servants, the servant may keep it until the year of freedom; then it will revert to the prince. His inheritance belongs to his sons only; it is theirs.

NIV Eze 46:18 The prince must not take any of the inheritance of the people, driving them off their property. He is to give his sons their inheritance out of his own property, so that none of my people will be separated from his property.' "

NIV Eze 46:19 Then the man brought me through the entrance at the side of the gate to the sacred rooms facing north, which belonged to the priests, and showed me a place at the western end.

NIV Eze 46:20 He said to me, "This is the place where the priests will cook the guilt offering and the sin offering and bake the grain offering, to avoid bringing them into the outer court and consecrating the people."

NIV Eze 46:21 He then brought me to the outer court and led me around to its four corners, and I saw in each corner another court.

NIV Eze 46:22 In the four corners of the outer court were enclosed courts, forty cubits long and thirty cubits wide; each of the courts in the four corners was the same size.

NIV Eze 46:23 Around the inside of each of the four courts was a ledge of stone, with places for fire built all around under the ledge.

NIV Eze 46:24 He said to me, "These are the kitchens where those who minister at the temple will cook the sacrifices of the people."

Finally, Ezekiel is told the boundaries of Israel, and the division of each of the twelve tribes and their geographical location in the nation; which gives them their status. As a part of their instructions, all the tribes are instructed to give land for the aliens who from the nations will come to reside in Israel. They are admonished to welcome them in as full citizens.

Finally, "the city" is described once more. Beginning with the positioning of the gates and the name of the city is finally told. This city, which is to belong to all of the nation of Israel, its capital (as it were) where the prince of the nation will reside and rule from. It is not as expected, and called Jerusalem any longer, nor is this natural city called the New Jerusalem, as one would expect. From this time forward the natural city,

Jerusalem, changes its name to, *Jehovah Shammah,* "THE LORD IS THERE". The name "Jerusalem" is now reserved for the celestial city, the New Jerusalem. It comes down from the heavenly realm, made of spiritual matter, and rests on the natural earth so that the Lord can cohabitate with mortal man.

The Gates of the City

NIV Eze 48:30 *"These will be the exits of the city: Beginning on the north side, which is 4,500 cubits long,*

NIV Eze 48:31 *the gates of the city will be named after the tribes of Israel. The three gates on the north side will be the gate of Reuben, the gate of Judah and the gate of Levi.*

NIV Eze 48:32 *"On the east side, which is 4,500 cubits long, will be three gates: the gate of Joseph, the gate of Benjamin and the gate of Dan.*

NIV Eze 48:33 *"On the south side, which measures 4,500 cubits, will be three gates: the gate of Simeon, the gate of Issachar and the gate of Zebulun.*

NIV Eze 48:34 *"On the west side, which is 4,500 cubits long, will be three gates: the gate of Gad, the gate of Asher and the gate of Naphtali.*

NIV Eze 48:35 *"The distance all around will be 18,000 cubits. "And the name of the city from that time on will be:*

"THE LORD IS THERE."

Through Ezekiel, we can have a realistic picture of what the millennium reign will look like. Israel is favored among the nations. The nations will still exist, however, what their names will be, how they will be divided up, into what kind of cultures after the battle of Armageddon, we do not know. We do know things will go back to basics. Technology and manufacturing will take a huge step backwards. There will be no need for it. It will be destroyed along with everything that is evil and amasses power and wealth for the few. Just as every city in the world will be destroyed.

People will not work for others making the few super wealthy, but in general everyone will have their own land, and grow their own food, and live peaceably among his fellows. People will live in harmony with each other. God will heal them, and individuals will get the aid they need to rebuild their lives into a semblance of peace, and self-sustenance. It will be by the aid of the celestial humans, living in their glorified bodies, as they are sent out to the nations to heal them.

The Lord Himself will settle all disputes; which will make it hard to deny the one God and seek after false gods. For God Himself will rule them. If they stray from acknowledging God and refuse to honor the Lord for who He is, He will impose sanctions on them, and not violence. He will not allow it to rain in their country and will cause them to suffer plagues. Their aid from the Lord will be cut off.

They will honor and serve the people of Israel; the ones God loves and favors! It will be a much different world to live in.

A few questions must be asked at this point:

Why is there a temple in the city? Revelation says there is no temple in the New Jerusalem. Besides, there is no need of it because the Lord and His Father are the temple. Their bodies are where their presence resides. Because it says:

> WEB Rev 22:4 *They will see his face, and his name will be on their foreheads. 5 There will be no night, and they need no lamp light; for the Lord God will illuminate them. They will reign forever and ever.*

Furthermore, why are the practices of temple worship of the Israelites revived? Sin has been paid for, Jesus has not only died on the cross, but has returned.

Why is the city called, "THE LORD IS THERE," and not, "The New Jerusalem?"
Why don't the measurements of anything in Ezekiel line up with the massive dimensions of the New Jerusalem in Revelation?

Lastly, where are the Christians, and what about their practices?

The answers for these questions are really quite elementary if we conceptually understand what these two different prophets are describing. Although they are talking about the same time period, the same location, and the same subject (the millennium reign of Christ), they are describing two different things on two different levels of existence. Let's look at this a little closer:

First of all, we must recall that the earth has moved from the natural universe to the spiritual realm where there is no sun.

WEB Rev 22:5 *There will be no night, and they need no lamp light; for the Lord God will illuminate them. They will reign forever and ever.*

The reason this shift of earth's location has happened is so God can make His dwelling with us. Furthermore, that means the mortal and the immortal will cohabitate. However, the mortals (who are made of natural matter) have much different environmental needs than those who are immortal (the celestial humans and angels). We can reconcile the differences between John and Ezekiel's prophetic picture of the millennium by recognizing, that Ezekiel's vision is one which views life in the millennium for mortal humans. Whereas John's Revelation is from the perspective of life in the millennium for celestial humans. One accounts for natural life, the other supernatural life, however, they are both speaking of the same time period and place on planet earth.

All the mortal Israelites will live in the nation of Israel. They will have as their capital, a city which is of natural matter named, THE LORD IS THERE. In that city there will be a temple which will house the Spirit of the Lord (His presence or His glory) and on occasion the Lord himself. The temple is needed so as to separate in the natural world a place which is Holy from the rest of the globe. There are walls all around the temple area, which separate this area from everywhere else, to keep the temple ground holy for the presence of the Lord.

We read in Ezekiel that many measures are taken in regard to the temple to keep it holy, separated, and undefiled by the condition of the rest of the world. Even though curses have been lifted off the earth, it doesn't mean the natural world has become purified and justified. On the contrary, we have already read how this earth and all that is of natural matter will be destroyed. As such, there are many accommodations made to allow the immortal and the mortal to co-exist. However, to be more accurate, that has been accomplished by the earth moving into the supernatural realm and bringing with it its atmosphere, the sky. The other accommodations made are for the holy to live among the unholy.

The New Jerusalem will also come down because it is the dwelling place of God. It is a supernatural city made of supernatural matter. Within the city will live all the supernatural beings including the celestial humans which will cohabitate on the earth with the living mortals in the earth.

Here is the understanding needed in order to have proper context: The New Jerusalem is a separate city from the natural city, THE LORD IS THERE (the old Jerusalem). In the New Jerusalem there is no need for a temple. Currently, our mortal bodies are the living breathing mobile temple of God that He embodies in the natural world. In the same manner, the celestial bodies of the Lord and His Father are the temple in the supernatural realm. The celestial humans who minister to them in the New Jerusalem will have a body in the same manner as Jesus and His Father. It is the celestial humans who will see His face, they will commune with Him, and stand before God.

Amp 1Co 13:12 For now we are looking in a mirror that gives only a dim (blurred) reflection [of reality as in a riddle or enigma], Now I know in part (imperfectly), but then I shall know and understand fully and clearly, even in the same manner as I have been fully and clearly known and understood [by God]

TLB 1 co 13:12 In the same way, we can see and understand only a little about God now, as if we were peering at his reflection in a poor mirror; but someday we are going to see him in his completeness, face-to-face. Now all that I know is hazy and blurred, but then I will see everything clearly, just as clearly as God sees into my heart right now.

What Paul says above (shown in two different translations) ". . . but then [when perfection comes] we shall see in reality and face-to-face!" becomes true for the celestial humans that reside in the New Jerusalem when the Lord returns to the earth.

Note: In reality, that happens when those in true *spiritual union* with the Lord die; or are raptured at the onset of the great tribulation; or at the time of the first resurrection. All of which depends on the circumstances of each individual. The mortal humans which live on the earth during that time will have to wait until the Last Day before that becomes true for them. That is to say, when they receive their resurrected/celestial body for the purpose of facing judgment and their eternal fate.

Until the Last Day, the mortal humans' perception of God will, as a rule, remain for them more of an experience of sensing the Lord's (overwhelming) presence. However, as in the days of Sodom and Gomorrah, the angels and celestial humans will be seen in a tangible way. Again, they will be seen by the mortals just as in the way the Devil, his angels, and the supernatural creatures from the abyss will be visibly seen, and able to physically torment, even kill the mortal humans. Until then, the mortal humans on earth during the reign of Christ will continue to perceive the Lord as though they are looking in a mirror that gives only a dim (blurred) reflection [of reality as in a riddle or enigma], in part (imperfectly). However, they will experience His radiance as the only source of light in the world and His overwhelming Spirit presence as the ultimate authority in the earth. Perhaps it will be that their eyes cannot see through or withstand the blinding radiance that comes from His person, in order to see His form.

It was said that nothing impure can enter the New Jerusalem. As such, the New Jerusalem is not a city in which mortal men can enter. It is only for the glorified ones.

How will these two cities be situated with each other? It does not say other than the New Jerusalem will sit on a mountain of supernatural ground. And it will be the chief of all the mountains on the earth. It also supersedes the city, THE LORD IS THERE, in size by many times over. It also says the New Jerusalem will be placed in the same area as the old Jerusalem.

Will they be side by side? Will they be stacked one on top of the other? Will the New Jerusalem hover over the earth and the city THE LORD IS THERE? A more reasonable understanding is that they will be layered in the same space like information on a blue ray disk that uses the same space with its information separated, by being on different frequencies. In the case of the two cities, seeing how one is celestial and the other natural, they can occupy the same space separated by dimensions instead of frequencies. In the case of a blue ray disk, the different layers of information occupy the same space because the information is stored on two different frequencies, and as such they can occupy the same space and not interfere with each other. The two different cities, likewise, consist of different kinds of matter and can thus, like a blue ray disk, occupy the same space.

We really are not told; however, Ezekiel gives us a big clue in the verses about the temple. The clue we find is in the River of Life. It transcends the New Jerusalem into the temple in the city of THE LORD IS THERE. Let's look again and see what it says:

NIV EZE 47:1 <u>Then he brought me back to the door of the house (Temple); and behold, water was flowing from under the threshold of the house toward the east, for the house faced east. And the water was flowing down from under, from the right side of the house, from south of the altar.</u>
NIV EZE 47:2 <u>He brought me out by way of the north gate and led me around on the outside to the outer gate by way of the gate that faces east. And behold, water was trickling from the south side.</u>

The angel is trying to bring to Ezekiel's attention the river, its source, then where it flows to.

NIV EZE 47:3 When the man went out toward the east with a line in his hand, he measured a thousand cubits, and he led me through the water, water reaching the ankles.
NIV EZE 47:4 Again he measured a thousand and led me through the water, water reaching the knees. Again he measured a thousand and led me through the water, water reaching the loins.
NIV EZE 47:5 Again he measured a thousand; and it was a river that I could not ford, for the water had risen, enough water to swim in, a river that could not be forded.
NIV EZE 47:6 He said to me, "Son of man, have you seen this?" Then he brought me back to the bank of the river.
NIV EZE 47:7 Now when I had returned, behold, on the bank of the river there were very many trees on the one side and on the other.
NIV EZE 47:8 Then he said to me, "These waters go out toward the eastern region and go down into the Arabah; then they go toward the sea, being made to flow into the sea, and the waters of the sea become fresh.
NIV EZE 47:9 "It will come about that every living creature which swarms in every place where the river goes, will live. And there will be very many fish, for these waters go there and the others become fresh; so everything will live where the river goes.
NIV EZE 47:10 "And it will come about that fishermen will stand beside it; from Engedi to Eneglaim there will be a place for the spreading of nets. Their fish will be according to their kinds, like the fish of the Great Sea, very many.
NIV EZE 47:11 "But its swamps and marshes will not become fresh; they will be left for salt.

NIV EZE 47:12 " By the river on its bank, on one side and on the other, will grow all kinds of trees for food. Their leaves will not wither and their fruit will not fail. They will bear every month because their water flows from the sanctuary, and their fruit will be for food and their leaves for healing."

This water leak, as it were, is trickling out from the River of Life in the supernatural city, the New Jerusalem. Its waters manifesting in the natural world of the earth from under the threshold of the temple in the natural city, THE LORD IS THERE. Gradually turning into a full-size river which is lined with all kinds of fruit bearing trees. It empties into the Dead Sea, causing it to no longer be lifeless. The angel shows Ezekiel many parts of it, even measuring it. Then says, "Son of man, have you seen this?" It is the angel's way of saying take special note of this. Why? No one could know its full meaning or its source until John had his Revelation thousands of years later. Until John, who gave the missing piece of the puzzle, the significance of the temple and the river in relation to the millennium has a mystery, however, if not for Ezekiel, we would never foreknow how the supernatural will co-exist with the natural.

John's Revelation from the perspective of the celestial realm:

WEB Rev 22:1 He showed me a river of water of life, clear as crystal, proceeding out of the throne of God and of the Lamb, 2 in the middle of its street. On this side of the river and on that was the tree of life, bearing twelve kinds of fruits, yielding its fruit every month. The leaves of the tree were for the healing of the nations.

In the supernatural city, the New Jerusalem, and from the throne of the Lord and His Father is the source of the River of Life. We see how in this city, the tree of life stands on both sides of the river. Then, the living waters from this river that flows from the throne of God somehow transcends from the supernatural to the natural. It flows into the temple in the natural city, THE LORD IS THERE. It flows from where His presence resides with His people and nation, Israel. It is said, whoever wants can drink from the River of Life and will never (spiritually) thirst again.

However, the source of the living waters that flow out of the natural temple is never revealed or asked about. It is not until 700 years later in Revelation that we can put it all together and understand why the angel was instructed to make Ezekiel take special note of the waters leaking in the temple. If not for Revelation, we would never know the source of this river, nor its importance. Neither would we see an example of how the natural and supernatural will cohabitate and interact with each other. To understand Revelation is to understand the Bible and its prophecy.

Note: In the beginning of this study we stated that to understand Revelation is paramount to understanding the whole Bible. We called Revelation the keys and framework by which to unlock the meaning of all prophecy. We are at the end of Revelation and we see this example of encryption personified with Ezekiel vs. Revelation. In Ezekiel's prophecy an angel brings special attention to something which would have escaped the attention of Ezekiel, or he would not have taken special note of otherwise. Without explanation of its true origin, the angel makes Ezekiel take very exacting notes about this water leaking and its benefit on the natural earth. Then, 700 years later, compelled by the Lord, John tells us the source. This is in keeping with what the angel told/showed Ezekiel what he did concerning the temple in the natural city "THE LORD IS THERE," when John later says, there is no temple.

Looking past the confusion, and having faith that their prophecy's do not contradict each other, together their prophecy's then help us understand that there are two cities which cohabitate with each other, one natural, one celestial, with two species of humans, one of natural matter, the other being celestial in nature. As a result, it is easy to judge the Bible as contradicting itself, unless one is thoughtful enough to homogenizing the entire collection of witnesses of prophecy in the Bible into a single context.

That context would be the understanding of the Good News of the Kingdom of God that Jesus came to spread. Jesus, who is the Son of God and the Son of Man, and the Spirit of prophecy who was given the scroll by the Father of all creation with its seven seals. Given so, He (the Lord), would communicate its content and redemptive alternative to us natural humans who are doomed as a species for destruction by the verdict of God. This messenger, Jesus Himself, is an enigma. His very nature is a seeming contradiction as to who and what He is, just as His message of salvation is.

Let us take a second look at the effects of this river of "living water." As it comes out of the temple in the city, THE LORD IS THERE, it is so filled with life that there will be a huge animal population prospering near its banks. Fruit trees and other plant life of every kind will line the banks of the River speaking of the life that is within the water. It will be so powerful that fruit bearing trees will bear fruit monthly instead of annually. And the leaves of these trees, as well as, the ones in the New Jerusalem, will have so much life in them from the water that they will be able to heal those who eat them (or lay them on their wounds). In fact, because there is so much life in the living waters, that we were told (above) the leaves will not go through a dormant season, Fall; meaning they will not turn brown and fall away.

The water is so powerful with life, it will take the Dead Sea and cause it to be filled with life, teeming in abundance with every kind of fish imaginable. This is water that brings life to everything it comes in contact with. Even if you touch or eat something that has grown from the water, it will heal you and bring life. This is an amazing, miraculous, and generous work of God in the world; because anyone can walk up to the river and drink from it freely. The only thing better would be to actually eat fruit from the Tree of Life that grows in the supernatural city, the New Jerusalem. Which, by the way, is watered by the same River.

The immortals who proceed out of the New Jerusalem where there is no temple, report directly to the Father and His Son. They see them on their thrones, in all of their glory. They behold their bodies, and speak to them face-to-face, and carry their words to the mortals outside of the city walls. But in the same place (in the natural, in the temple of the city THE LORD IS THERE), the prince of Israel and the high priest bring the offerings to a room where the very presence of the Lord is there in power. There, they commune with Him via His presence, His Spirit. However, in the very same place in a different dimension, the person of the Lord sits on His throne and those who are called His bride and have their glorified bodies, speak face-to-face with Him. These celestial humans, His bride, are a kingdom of priests ministering to the Lord and over the mortals of the earth.

NIV Rev 5:10 You have made them to be a kingdom and priests to serve our God, and they will reign on the earth."

The next thing to address is the fact that temple worship is revived, the original practices of the Israelites, and not the practices of the Christians. If these practices are resumed during this time, it needs to be assumed that the temple worship does not negate the redeeming work Jesus did on the cross. The Christian practices have come to their end. The fate of every single Christ follower has been determined.

They have either:

- Received their celestial body before the head of their natural body hit the ground in death.
- Were caught up to heaven, receiving their celestial body at the rapture during the onset of the great tribulation.
- Were raised from the dead in the days before the seventh trumpet. Then raptured and given a celestial body along with those who survived the great tribulation and had endured it without abandoning their testimony.
- A disembodied soul in the paradisiacal place of Hades, awaiting the last day when all the dead will receive a celestial body and then be judged a sheep.
- Or a disembodied soul in the hellish place of Hades having lost their salvation. Then given a celestial body on the Last Day subsequently being judged a goat and thrown alive, into the lake of fire suffering a second death.

The Israelites/Jews, however, had rejected their Christ. They (the first, who as a result, are last) have lost their place as "the bride." That is to be the celestial humans who were to come with Christ at His second coming to serve Him as priests and rule the earth with Him. There was a pause in the 70-7's God decreed for them in order to position them to be His bride of celestial humans. In fact, this pause started at the close of the 69th seven, and before the last or 70th seven. This pause is the Church Age, a time for the Lord to make a bride for Himself because those who that place was reserved for, rejected it.

At this point in the story, the Church Age is complete. The search for a bride which made the last first, put the Gentile world in front of His beloved Israel, taking their role. Everything for the Christians/Gentiles has been determined, completed and accounted for to the last Christian. The 70-7's both resumed and came to a conclusion. This 1,000-year reign is for all the unfinished business (as it were) of the plan and promises of God to be fulfilled to the letter. It is for the mortal Israelites and Jews. It is to be the time to have all the promises of God that He made to their patriarchs, fulfilled. It only stands to reason that in bringing to a close the plan of God for His beloved Israel, which was temporarily paused, He will resume temple worship as was their custom and way to connect with the Lord.

All throughout the writings of Ezekiel, the Lord reminds the Israelites that He is not doing this for them because of any effort they have made on their part, but to keep His name holy, which they profaned among the nations they were sent to. The Lord promises to put in them a new Spirit which will cause them to finally follow Him. That is in keeping with the New Covenant promises Christ followers received. However, when He does so He says, they will be ashamed because they will remember their sins, and in essence, be reminded how God had to do it all. By their actions and pursuits, they failed to deserve the love God has lavished on them, however, for the sake of what He promised to their forefathers, who were God's friends, He does as He committed to do in spite of them.

Ezekiel showed us that the very way the temple is designed is to remind them of this shame during the millennium. Not to rub their nose in it so they don't enjoy the time for them to shine, but to keep them sober, humble, and living in the truth of how gracious their God is. The temple practices are now used to remind them what they were, and to cause them to be humble and submitted to their God. And not for the purposes of looking forward to salvation to come, salvation cohabitates with them during this time.

Finally, where are the Christians? Where are their practices (which presumably surpassed and dated those of the Jews and their temple worship)? This is where reality sinks in! We ask the Church, have you been listening to the message of this Revelation? This message is to you!

Although the message of Revelation is to us, the Christians, this story which spans thousands of years, is not our story. It never was. It is the story of the Israelites and the God of Abraham, Isaac, and Jacob. It is the story of the two different lines of offspring. It is not the story of the Church! Every promise God made to Eve through the children of Abraham has its fulfillment in the millennium reign and beyond.

Fulfillment for the Christians happens during the Church Age. That is from the time we, the Gentiles, killed the Lord until the rapture. It is the time period allotted by the Father because the Christ said:

WEB Lk 23:34 Jesus said, "Father, forgive them, for they don't know what they are doing." Dividing his garments among them, they cast lots. 35 The people stood watching. The rulers with them also scoffed at him, saying, "He saved others. Let him save himself, if this is the Christ of God, his chosen one!"

The Church Age is the gap or delay that precedes the 70th-7. The 70-7's which were decreed for the Israelites, and not the world. However, the Church Age—the gap between the 69th and 70th or final seven—is the age of pardon and the age where the enemies of God can be forgiven and absorbed into His people before He destroys them. It is a departure from the redeeming work done for the Israelites because of their rejection of their Lord. It is the gathering of everyone in the streets to fill up the house for the wedding, which was ready, and the ones who were invited did not answer the call, while rejecting their host. We Christians are the Roman centurion who after killing the Lord of Glory said:

WEB Mk 15:39 When the centurion, who stood by opposite him, saw that he cried out like this and breathed his last, he said, "Truly this man was the Son of God!"

We are the ones who did not know Him or follow Him, we were not His people, we are the ones who seduced His people away from Him because of our ways. But by grace and mercy, we are the ones who have become first, while the first have become last.

Anyone who wants to be reconciled to God in the millennium Kingdom will have to be absorbed by the Israelites, whether or not they think themselves of Christian heritage or some heathen religion. The Church has become about the individuals in it. And the Church itself will be utterly destroyed never to rise up again. This is the fate of the Church:

WEB Rev 17:16 *The ten horns which you saw, and the beast, these will hate the prostitute, <u>and will</u>* <u>make her desolate, and will make her naked, and will eat her flesh, and will burn her utterly</u> <u>with fire.</u>

There will be nothing left of it. It will be destroyed forever. Even in the letters to the Church, Jesus says the same thing of her. Only individuals within her will be saved. The *Church Corrupt* is Babylon. We think too highly of ourselves as a group and a people. The status, influence, power, and wealth the Church has in the world was directly given to her by the beast and his kingdom, the Roman Empire. Or eventually was by recreating and ruling the fallen Roman Empire for reasons of its own power and wealth. More importantly, not by God, as we might have mistakenly assumed. The Church has become Rome. It has sold out! It sits on a pedestal, thinking it is the exception and can do no wrong and it is above everyone else in the earth. It thinks too highly of itself:

NIV Rev 18:7 *Give her as much torture and grief as the glory and luxury she gave herself. <u>In her</u>* <u>heart she boasts, 'I sit as queen; I am not a widow, and I will never mourn.'</u>

In regard to verse 7 (below), it says in Daniel something quite different than what the *Church Corrupt* says about herself:

WEB Da 12:7 *I heard the man clothed in linen, who was above the waters of the river, when he held up his right hand and his left hand to heaven, and swore by him who lives forever that it will be for a time, times, and a half; and <u>when they have finished breaking in pieces the power of</u>* <u>the holy people, all these things will be finished.</u>

Those Christians who were actually and truly the body of Christ, the outward expression of His Spirit within them, they are taken up with His Spirit that withdraws from the earth for 3-1/2 years. They, His body, return to the earth with Him now being the celestial humans that reside with Him in the New Jerusalem. They, likewise, co-rule the earth along with those who held true to their profession of faith during the great tribulation. However, the Church is burnt down to the ground. Both its time and purpose fulfilled. The Church Age was a grace, and when it comes to its end, the Lord then turns His attention and grace back to the two sisters He loved from the beginning, Israel and Judah.

NIV Jer 3:1 *"If a man divorces his wife*
and she leaves him and marries another man,
should he return to her again?
Would not the land be completely defiled?
But you have lived as a prostitute with many lovers—
would you now return to me?"
declares the LORD.
NIV Jer 3:2 *"Look up to the barren heights and see.*
Is there any place where you have not been ravished?
By the roadside you sat waiting for lovers,
sat like a nomad in the desert.
You have defiled the land
with your prostitution and wickedness.
NIV Jer 3:3 *Therefore the showers have been withheld,*
and no spring rains have fallen.
Yet you have the brazen look of a prostitute;
you refuse to blush with shame.
NIV Jer 3:4 *Have you not just called to me:*
'My Father, my friend from my youth,
NIV Jer 3:5 *will you always be angry?*
Will your wrath continue forever?'
This is how you talk,
but you do all the evil you can."

NIV Jer 3:6 *During the reign of King Josiah, the LORD said to me, "Have you seen what faithless Israel has done? She has gone up on every high hill and under every spreading tree and has committed adultery there.*
NIV Jer 3:7 *I thought that after she had done all this she would return to me but she did not, and her unfaithful sister Judah saw it.*
NIV Jer 3:8 *I gave faithless Israel her certificate of divorce and sent her away because of all her adulteries. Yet I saw that her unfaithful sister Judah had no fear; she also went out and committed adultery.*
NIV Jer 3:9 *Because Israel's immorality mattered so little to her, she defiled the land and committed adultery with stone and wood.*

NIV Jer 3:10 In spite of all this, her unfaithful sister Judah <u>did not return to me with all her heart,</u>
<u>*but only in pretense," declares the LORD.*</u>
NIV Jer 3:11 The LORD said to me, "Faithless Israel is more righteous than unfaithful Judah.
NIV Jer 3:12 Go, proclaim this message toward the north:
" 'Return, faithless Israel,' declares the LORD,
<u>*'I will frown on you no longer,*</u>
<u>*for I am merciful,' declares the LORD,*</u>
<u>*'I will not be angry forever.*</u>
NIV Jer 3:13 <u>Only acknowledge your guilt—</u>
<u>*you have rebelled against the LORD your God,*</u>
you have scattered your favors to foreign gods
under every spreading tree,
and have not obeyed me,' "
declares the LORD.

Although the Lord started this oracle saying: "If a man divorces his wife and she leaves him and marries another man, should he return to her again? Would not the land be completely defiled? But you have lived as a prostitute with many lovers—would you now return to me?" declares the LORD. Should a woman who divorced her husband and took another return to him?" By any standards these circumstances would be a further or double humiliation to the husband to take back the unfaithful wife who defiled herself and her marriage. In fact, it says above it defiles the land or more specifically, the home/household. Although turning Israel and Judah away and punishing her by her lovers, in the end, the Lord's love for her wins out as we see below.

Jer 3:14 "Return, faithless people," declares the LORD, "for I am your husband. <u>I will choose you—</u>
<u>*one from a town and two from a clan—and bring you to Zion.*</u>
Jer 3:15 <u>Then I will give you shepherds after my own heart, who will lead you with knowledge</u>
<u>*and understanding.*</u>
Jer 3:16 In those days, when your numbers have increased greatly in the land," declares the LORD,
"men will no longer say, 'The ark of the covenant of the LORD.' It will never enter their minds
or be remembered; it will not be missed, nor will another one be made.
Jer 3:17 At that time they will call Jerusalem The Throne of the LORD, and all nations will gather
in Jerusalem to honor the name of the LORD. No longer will they follow the stubbornness of
their evil hearts.

Jer 3:18 *In those days the house of Judah will join the house of Israel, and together they will come*
from a northern land to the land I gave your forefathers as an inheritance.
Jer 3:19 *"I myself said,*
"'How gladly would I treat you like sons
and give you a desirable land,
the most beautiful inheritance of any nation.'
I thought you would call me 'Father'
and not turn away from following me.
Jer 3:20 *But like a woman unfaithful to her husband,*
so you have been unfaithful to me, O house of Israel,"
declares the LORD.

Jer 3:21 *A cry is heard on the barren heights,*
the weeping and pleading of the people of Israel,
because they have perverted their ways
and have forgotten the LORD their God.

Jer 3:22 *"Return, faithless people;*
I will cure you of backsliding."

"Yes, we will come to you,
for you are the LORD our God.

The Church has taken Jerusalem away from God's people the Israelites,
during the Crusades. Babylon in the Church has murdered, burned, tortured,
starved, and band them from their homeland. Just as Babylon/Rome did to them. The
Church has looked down on them and despised them and has taken what was not theirs
but was the Israelites. The *Church Corrupt* committed the crime of Esau and Tyre.
Even though we forget, the Lord's jealous love burns for them, as a result, and as with
Esau and Tyre, the Lord's jealousy burns against us.

Jesus is not just talking about the Roman Catholic Church. He is talking about the
Church as a whole. This is not a doom and gloom message of our own making, this is
the story that is told by the Spirit of prophecy. Remember what Jesus says in the seven

letters to the seven churches. Listen to what Paul says about this very subject. He says it to Rome. It was prophetic! How could Paul know in that very city, everything he warned them about was what they, in the future, needed to hear?

God's sovereign choice

WEB Ro 9:1 I tell the truth in Christ. I am not lying, my conscience testifying with me in the Holy Spirit, 2 that I have great sorrow and unceasing pain in my heart. 3 For I could wish that I myself were accursed from Christ for my brothers' sake, my relatives according to the flesh, 4 who are Israelites; whose is the adoption, the glory, the covenants, the giving of the law, the service, and the promises; 5 of whom are the fathers, and from whom is Christ as concerning the flesh, who is over all, God, blessed forever. Amen. 6 But it is not as though the word of God has come to nothing. For they are not all Israel, that are of Israel. 7 Neither, because they are Abraham's offspring, are they all children. But, "your offspring will be accounted (reconciled) as from Isaac." 8 That is, it is not the children of the flesh who are children of God, but the children of the promise are counted as heirs. 9 For this is a word of promise, "At the appointed time I will come, and Sarah will have a son." 10 Not only so, but Rebekah also conceived by one, by our father Isaac. 11 For being not yet born, neither having done anything good or bad, that the purpose of God according to election might stand, not of works, but of him who calls, 12 it was said to her, "The elder will serve the younger." 13 Even as it is written, "Jacob I loved, but Esau I hated." 14 What shall we say then? Is there unrighteousness with God? May it never be! 15 For he said to Moses, "I will have mercy on whom I have mercy, and I will have compassion on whom I have compassion." 16 So then it is not of him who wills, nor of him who runs, but of God who has mercy. 17 For the Scripture says to Pharaoh, "For this very purpose I caused you to be raised up, that I might show in you my power, and that my name might be proclaimed in all the earth." 18 So then, he has mercy on whom he desires, and he hardens whom he desires. 19 You will say then to me, "Why does he still find fault? For who withstands his will?" 20 But indeed, O man, who are you to reply against God? Will the thing formed ask him who formed it, "Why did you make me like this?" 21 Or hasn't the potter a right over the clay, from the same lump to make one part a vessel for honor, and another for dishonor? 22 What if God, willing to show his wrath, and to make his power known, endured with much patience vessels of wrath made for destruction, 23 and that he might make known the riches of his glory on vessels of mercy, which he prepared beforehand for glory, 24 us, whom he also called, not from the Jews only, but also from the Gentiles? 25 As he says also in Hosea, "I will call them 'my people,' which were not my people; and her 'beloved,' who was not beloved." [26] "It will be that in the place where it was said to them, 'You are not my people,' There they will be called 'children of the living God.'" [27] Isaiah cries concerning Israel, "If the number of the children of Israel are as the sand of the sea, it is the remnant who will be saved; [28] for He will finish the work and cut it short in righteousness, because the LORD will make a short work upon the earth." [29] As Isaiah has said before, "Unless the Lord of Armies had left us a seed, we would have become like Sodom, and would have been made like Gomorrah.

Paul is referring to the fact that God will bring back Israel to form a nation during the millennium not because they deserved it, but to keep His word and His name holy. If not, they would be as Sodom and Gomorrah, utterly destroyed. But through that single seed, Jesus, they will be like the sands of the sea.

Israel's Unbelief

WEB Ro 9:30 What shall we say then? That the Gentiles, who didn't follow after righteousness, attained to righteousness, even the righteousness which is of faith; [31] but Israel, following after a law of righteousness, didn't arrive at the law of righteousness. [32] Why? Because they didn't seek it by faith, but as it were by works of the law. They stumbled over the stumbling stone; [33] even as it is written, "Behold, I lay in Zion a stumbling stone and a rock of offense; and no one who believes in him will be disappointed." WEB Ro 10:1 Brothers, my heart's desire and my prayer to God is for Israel, that they may be saved. [2] For I testify about them that they have a zeal for God, but not according to knowledge. [3] For being ignorant of God's righteousness, and seeking to establish their own righteousness, they didn't subject themselves to the righteousness of God. [4] For Christ is the fulfillment of the law for righteousness to everyone who believes. [5] For Moses writes about the righteousness of the law, "The one who does them will live by them." [6] But the righteousness which is of faith says this, "Don't say in your heart, 'Who will ascend into heaven?' (that is, to bring Christ down); [7] or, 'Who will descend into the abyss?' (that is, to bring Christ up from the dead.)" [8] But what does it say? "The word is near you, in your mouth, and in your heart"; that is, the word of faith, which we preach: [9] that if you will confess with your mouth that Jesus is Lord, and believe in your heart that God raised him from the dead, you will be saved. [10] For with the heart, one believes unto righteousness; and with the mouth confession is made unto salvation. [11] For the Scripture says, "Whoever believes in him will not be disappointed." [12] For there is no distinction between Jew and Greek; for the same

Lord is Lord of all, and is rich to all who call on him. *[13]* For, "Whoever will call on the name of the Lord will be saved." *[14]* How then will they call on him in whom they have not believed? How will they believe in him whom they have not heard? How will they hear without a preacher? *[15]* And how will they preach unless they are sent? As it is written: "How beautiful are the feet of those who preach the Good News of peace, who bring glad tidings of good things!" *[16]* But they didn't all listen to the glad news. For Isaiah says, "Lord, who has believed our report?" *[17]* So faith comes by hearing, and hearing by the word of God. *[18]* But I say, didn't they hear? Yes, most certainly, "Their sound went out into all the earth, their words to the ends of the world. *[19]* But I ask, didn't Israel know? First Moses says, "I will provoke you to jealousy with that which is no nation, with a nation void of understanding I will make you angry." *[20]* Isaiah is very bold, and says, "I was found by those who didn't seek me. I was revealed to those who didn't ask for me." *[21]* But as to Israel he says, "All day long I stretched out my hands to a disobedient and contrary people."

The Remnant of Israel

WEB Ro 11:1 I ask then, did God reject his people? May it never be! For I also am an Israelite, a descendant of Abraham, of the tribe of Benjamin. *[2]* God didn't reject his people, which he foreknew. Or don't you know what the Scripture says about Elijah? How he pleads with God against Israel: *[3]* "Lord, they have killed your prophets, they have broken down your altars; and I am left alone, and they seek my life." *[4]* But how does God answer him? "I have reserved for myself seven thousand men, who have not bowed the knee to Baal." *[5]* Even so then at this present time also there is a remnant according to the election of grace. *[6]* And if by grace, then it is no longer of works; otherwise grace is no longer grace. But if it is of works, it is no longer grace; otherwise work is no longer work. *[7]* What then? That which Israel seeks for, that he didn't obtain, but the chosen ones obtained it, and the rest were hardened. *[8]* According as it is written, "God gave them a spirit of stupor, eyes that they should not see, and ears that they should not hear, to this very day." *[9]* David says, "Let their table be made a snare, and a trap, a stumbling block, and a retribution to them. *[10]* Let their eyes be darkened, that they may not see. Bow down their back always."

Ingrafted Branches

WEB Ro 11:11 I ask then, did they stumble that they might fall? May it never be! But by their fall salvation has come to the Gentiles, to provoke them to jealousy. *[12]* Now if their fall is the riches of the world, and their loss the riches of the Gentiles; how much more their fullness? *13 For I speak to you who are Gentiles. Since then as I am an apostle to Gentiles, I glorify my ministry; 14 if by any means I may provoke to jealousy those who are my flesh, and may save some of them. 15 For if the rejection of them is the reconciling of the world, what would their acceptance be, but life from the dead? 16 If the first fruit is holy, so is the lump. If the root is holy, so are the branches. 17 But if some of the branches were broken off, and you, being a wild olive, were grafted in among them, and became partaker with them of the root and of the richness of the olive tree; 18 don't boast over the branches. But if you boast, it is not you who support the root, but the root supports you. 19 You will say then, "Branches were broken off, that I might be grafted in." 20 True; by their unbelief they were broken off, and you stand by your faith. Don't be conceited, but fear; 21 for if God didn't spare the natural branches, neither will he spare you. 22 See then the goodness and severity of God. Toward those who fell, severity; but toward you, goodness, if you continue in his goodness; otherwise you also will be cut off. 23 They also, if they don't continue in their unbelief, will be grafted in, for God is able to graft them in again. 24 For if you were cut out of that which is by nature a wild olive tree, and were grafted contrary to nature into a good olive tree, how much more will these, which are the natural branches, be grafted into their own olive tree?*

All Israel Will Be Saved

WEB Ro 11:25 *For I don't desire you to be ignorant, brothers, of this mystery, so that you won't be wise in your own conceits, that a partial hardening has happened to Israel, until the fullness of the Gentiles has come in, 26 and so all Israel will be saved. Even as it is written, "There will come out of Zion the Deliverer, and he will turn away ungodliness from Jacob. 27 This is my covenant to them, when I will take away their sins." 28 Concerning the Good News, they are enemies for your sake. But concerning the election, they are beloved for the fathers' sake. 29 For the gifts and the calling of God are irrevocable. 30 For as you in time past were disobedient to God, but now have obtained mercy by their disobedience, 31 even so these also have now been disobedient, that by the mercy shown to you they may also obtain mercy. 32 For God has shut up all to disobedience, that he might have mercy on all* (alike).

Doxology

WEB Ro 11:33 Oh the depth of the riches both of the wisdom and the knowledge of God! How unsearchable are his judgments, and his ways past tracing out! [34] *"For who has known the mind of the Lord? Or who has been his counselor?"* [35] *"Or who has first given to him, and it will be repaid to him again?"* [36] *For of him, and through him, and to him, are all things. To him be the glory for ever! Amen.*

Living Sacrifices

WEB Ro 12:1 Therefore I urge you, brothers, by the mercies of God, to present your bodies a living sacrifice, holy, acceptable to God, which is your spiritual service (This means to live in spiritual union with Christ and to die to your own life, which is spiritual worship) [2] *Don't be conformed to this world, but be transformed by the renewing of your mind, so that you may prove what is the good, well-pleasing, and perfect will of God.* [3] *For I say, through the grace that was given me, to every man who is among you, not to think of himself more highly than he ought to think; but to think reasonably, as God has apportioned to each person a measure of faith.*

Esau He hated and Jacob He loved. Why? Both were evil in nature. Jacob's name means deceiver or usurper. He operated out of jealousy and deceit. They both were deserving of wrath, both from the same lump of clay. However, Esau wanted worldly power and physical strength. Whereas Jacob by faith wanted the spiritual promise and what the Lord had. We are not saved because we are better than the first born, the Israelites. But because by faith we want the promise, and not the power and physical strength of this world.

Jacob loved Rachael but because of her father had to marry Leah first, and had also to wait and work for another seven years (completion and perfection) to pay the price to have the one he really loved, Rachael. The Father has asked Jesus, His Son, to marry us the Gentiles, Leah, the one He did not love. But because of the time of the Church Age He must work for His Father another 2,000-years, so that He can finally, after the Church Age, have His Rachel, the Israelites, and be with them in His Kingdom forever!

Wake Up O'Sleepers! Come out of the Church and into His Body! The time of reckoning and subsequent gathering to the bosom of the Lord's, despite our unfaithfulness (the prostituting of ourselves to Babylon), is at hand! It comes for the Church in the form of the great tribulation. It will happen in its entirety before He turns His heart back towards his beloved Judah and Israel. Why? Because the last has become the first, but make no mistake, He has not forgotten those whose names He tattooed on His hand.

Below is a dialogue between Mount Zion and the Lord. Mount Zion laments to the Lord that her children (the Israelites) have been carried away and are no more. However, the Lord comforts Mount Zion and tells her how her children, the Israelites, will return to her and Zion will burst at the seams with all of the children of Israel that will return to her. He says the Israelites will populate you (Zion) and be as ornaments upon you (as ornaments on a tree).

ZION: *NIV Isa 49:14 But Zion said, "The LORD has forsaken me,*

the Lord has forgotten me."

THE LORD: *NIV Isa 49:15 "Can a mother forget the baby at her breast*

and have no compassion on the child she has borne?

Though she may forget,

I will not forget you!

NIV Isa 49:16 <u>*See, I have engraved you on the palms of my hands;*</u>

<u>*your walls are ever before me.*</u>

NIV Isa 49:17 Your (Zion's) *sons hasten back,*

and those who laid you (Zion) *waste depart from you.*

NIV Isa 49:18 Lift up your (Zion's) *eyes and look around;*

all your sons gather and come to you.

As surely as I live," declares the LORD,

"you will wear them all as ornaments;

you will put them (Israelites) *on, like a bride.*

NIV Isa 49:19 "*Though you* (Zion) *were ruined and made desolate*
and your land laid waste,
now you will be too small for your people (Israel),
and those (Babylon) *who devoured you will be far away.*
NIV Isa 49:20 The children born during your bereavement
will yet say in your hearing,

All of the diaspora—the people in the world of Jewish and Israeli descent who were exiled out of Mount Zion—it is their children who were born in exile during Zion's bereavement. They are generations of children born after Babylon exiled them. Zion is astonished at their numbers when the Lord calls them to return.

THE RETURNED ISRAELITES: 'This place is too small for us;

give us more space to live in.'
NIV Isa 49:21 Then you (Zion) *will say in your heart,*
ZION: *'Who bore me these?*

I was bereaved and barren;
I was exiled and rejected.
Who brought these up (Who raised them)*?*
I was left all alone,
but these—where have they come from?'"
Isa 49:22 This is what the Sovereign LORD says:
THE LORD: "*See, I will beckon to the Gentiles,*

I will lift up my banner to the peoples;
they will bring your sons in their arms
and carry your daughters on their shoulders.
NIV Isa 49:23 Kings will be your foster fathers,
and their queens your nursing mothers.
They will bow down before you with their faces to the ground;
they will lick the dust at your feet.
Then you will know that I am the LORD?
those who hope in me will not be disappointed."

NIV Isa 49:24 Can plunder be taken from warriors,
or captives rescued from the fierce?

NIV Isa 49:25 But this is what the LORD says:
"Yes, captives will be taken from warriors,
and plunder retrieved from the fierce;
I will contend with those who contend with you,
and your children I will save.
NIV Isa 49:26 I will make your oppressors eat their own flesh;
they will be drunk on their own blood, as with wine.
Then all mankind will know
that I, the LORD, am your Savior,
your Redeemer, the Mighty One of Jacob."

In closing, the vision of the New Jerusalem: It was said as in all visions from God that within it, you can see the beginning and the end of the subject matter. The subject matter of this vision is, of course, the New Jerusalem. However, in this case, the subject of this vision has no end. It was made eternal and is eternal. We are told about it in the vision only as far as the story of the scroll with seven seals takes us. This vision does not describe the transition from being on the natural earth to the eternities. That is because it was never part of or constructed of matter from the natural universe where the earth and man come from. It has always and forever belonged to the heavens and the Father. Its occupants are the same from the beginning as they are in the end—the end which does not exist nor ever comes.

WEB Rev 22:3 There will be no curse anymore. The throne of God and of the Lamb will be in it (the city), and his servants (celestial humans) serve him. 4 They will see his face, and his name will be on their foreheads. 5 There will be no night, and they need no lamp light; for the Lord God will illuminate them. They will reign forever and ever.

CHAPTER 5

Jesus is Coming

WEB Rev 22:6 He said to me, "These words are faithful and true. The Lord God of the spirits of the prophets sent his angel to show to his bondservants the things which must happen soon."

His Father had spoken. Now that all is said and done Jesus, the Spirit of prophecy, is taking this opportunity to give us His assurance and admonishment. These words of His are a message to all of His Church, both the *Church Pure* and the *Church Corrupt*. He speaks to them now that He has told everything that will take place that He is released by the Father to tell us. Though His words are few, they are profound, powerful, and decisive. It could be understood that He keeps them few so as not to take away from what His Father already spoke after the vision of the Dead are Judged.

WEB Rev 22:7 "Behold, I come quickly. Blessed is he who keeps the words of the prophecy of this book."

Finally, John, the one who took this message down, says his closing words, as well. In them he gives his witness to their authenticity.

WEB Rev 22:8 Now I, John, am the one who heard and saw these things. When I heard and saw, I fell down to worship before the feet of the angel who had shown me these things. 9 He said to me, "See you don't do it! I am a fellow bondservant with you and with your brothers, the prophets, and with those who keep the words of this book. Worship God." 10 He said to me, "Don't seal up the words of the prophecy of this book, for the time is at hand. 11 He who acts unjustly, let him act unjustly still. He who is filthy, let him be filthy still. He who is righteous, let him do righteousness still. He who is holy, let him be holy still."

This is how Daniel's vision ended, he was told also, that many will go to and fro gaining wisdom and be purified, but the wicked will continue to be wicked. They will not heed these words and save themselves. The difference is, John is asked not to seal up the words because the time is near, whereas Daniel was asked to seal them up because it concerned the distant future.

WEB Rev 22:12 *"Behold, I come quickly. My reward is with me, to repay to each man according to his work. ¹³ I am the Alpha and the Omega, the First and the Last, the Beginning and the End. ¹⁴ Blessed are those who do his commandments, that they may have the right to the tree of life, and may enter in by the gates into the city. ¹⁵ Outside are the dogs, the sorcerers, the sexually immoral, the murderers, the idolaters, and everyone who loves and practices falsehood. ¹⁶ I, Jesus, have sent my angel to testify these things to you for the assemblies* (churches). *I am the root and the offspring of David; the Bright and Morning Star." ¹⁷ The Spirit and the bride say, "Come!" He who hears, let him say, "Come!" He who is thirsty, let him come. He who desires, let him take the water of life freely. ¹⁸ I testify to everyone who hears the words of the prophecy of this book, if anyone adds to them, may God add to him the plagues which are written in this book. ¹⁹ If anyone takes away from the words of the book of this prophecy, may God take away his part from the tree of life, and out of the holy city, which are written in this book. ²⁰ He who testifies these things says, "Yes, I come quickly." Amen! Yes, come, Lord Jesus. ²¹ The grace of the Lord Jesus Christ be with all the saints. Amen.*

Amen!

Bibliography

Amplified Bible. Scripture quotations marked (AMP) are taken from the Amplified Bible, Copyright © 1954, 1958, 1962, 1964, 1965, 1987 by The Lockman Foundation. Used by permission.

Baring-Gould, S. (1871) *Legends of Old Testament Characters, from the Talmud and other sources.* London: R. Clay, Sons, and Taylor, Printers.

Farabee, Mike (2001). Retrieved December 2019, from Estrella Mountain Community College: https://www2.estrellamountain.edu/faculty/farabee/biobk/BioBookEner1.html

New American Standard. Scripture quotations marked (NAS) are taken from the NEW AMERICAN STANDARD BIBLE®, Copyright © 1960,1962,1963,1968,1971,1972,1973,1975,1977,1995 by The Lockman Foundation. Used by permission.

New International Version. Scriptures taken from the Holy Bible, New International Version®, NIV®. Copyright © 1973, 1978, 1984 by Biblica, Inc.™ Used by permission of Zondervan. All rights reserved worldwide. www.zondervan.com The "NIV" and "New International Version" are trademarks registered in the United States Patent and Trademark Office by Biblica, Inc.™

New Revised Standard Version Bible (NRSV), copyright © 1989 National Council of the Churches of Christ in the United States of America. Used by permission. All rights reserved worldwide.

The Living Bible. Scripture quotations marked (TLB) are taken from The Living Bible copyright © 1971. Used by permission of Tyndale House Publishers, a Division of Tyndale House Ministries, Carol Stream, Illinois 60188. All rights reserved.

The Voice. Scripture taken from The Voice™. Copyright © 2012 by Ecclesia Bible Society. Used by permission. All rights reserved.

World English Bible. Scripture quotations marked (WEB) are taken from The World English Bible, which is in the public domain. Special thanks to Michael Paul Johnson and all who worked on the translation as a means to release a modern version of the Bible that is available for non-copyright use. A reminder that the Bible is not owned by man.

ABOUT THE AUTHORS

We are just a voice

WEB Jn 1:19 This is John's testimony (about himself), when the Jews sent priests and Levites from Jerusalem to ask him, "Who are you?"

WEB Jn 1:20 *He declared, and didn't deny, but he declared, "I am not the Christ."*

WEB Jn 1:21 *They asked him, "What then? Are you Elijah?"*

He said, "I am not."

"Are you the prophet?"

He answered, "No."

WEB Jn 1:22 *They said therefore to him, "Who are you? Give us an answer to take back to those who sent us. What do you say about yourself?"*

WEB Jn 1:23 *He said, "**I am the voice** of one crying in the wilderness, 'Make straight the way of the Lord . . ."*

True prophets in the Bible did not convince people who they were; in fact, they refused to talk about themselves. They refused to bring credibility to the words of God they spoke by trying to get people to believe who they were and trust them. They knew that it would be profaning the words of God to do so, and it would be elevating themselves above God's words. They knew that God's words have their own credibility because they are from God. And God will show them (His own words) as from Him.

God's prophets also knew that those who truly love God will, therefore, benefit from their words, and those who are lovers of themselves will not benefit from them, because they will be dismissive and not trust them. The time is over that we look at the person who speaks to decide if we believe. We must begin to discern if the words are from God and if they carry God's Spirit.

You might say to that, "but not everyone can discern God." If that is the case, then they indict themselves as not being "known" by Jesus. They unwittingly reveal about themselves that they desire to do their own will and not the Lord's, just as the religious leaders who wanted Jesus to prove His credibility so they could decide if His words were from God.

Amp Jn 7:16 Jesus answered them by saying, My teaching is not My own, but His Who sent Me. Amp Jn 7:17 If any man desires to do His will (God's pleasure), he will know (have the needed illumination to recognize, and can tell for himself) whether the teaching is from God or whether I am speaking from Myself and of My own accord and on My own authority.

Many will think this is an oversimplified notion. However, it is so simple that it is not only true but reveals a simple but foundational truth about the person. What Jesus is saying is that if a man has a pure heart and wants to do the will of God above his own will, then what seems intuitively right (what sets well with that man) will be God's will and His words. However, even if you are a scholar, theologian, or work in the field of religion, and you desire to carry out your own will, having your own agendas and ambitions, well then, what seems right to that man is not God's will or His words, but that which lines up with his own will.

Generally speaking, the greatest religious minds in the world judge if something is from God by looking at the standing and qualifications of the man speaking them. In the above case, Jesus shows they may be smart in their own eyes, believing they know what is from God and therefore able to judge according to their knowledge of God. However, that would be saying in effect, we know everything about God because of our great knowledge. Therefore, if you say anything outside of our knowledge of God, or outside of the knowledge base of the accepted theological models, or if you are not a qualified student of those accepted models, then we must deduce your words are not from God.

To Jesus, they show about themselves that they don't recognize His words as from God because of their personal acquaintance with God. Instead, they have to judge by facts. They show themselves as having no real relationship with God; they would not recognize Him when He stands right before them. As a matter of fact, on another occasion when they showed contempt for Him, Jesus said of them:

NIV Jn 5:42 ... *but I know you. I know that you do not have the love of God in your hearts.*

They were once again wanting Him to prove who He was, and what right He had to talk the way He did. Jesus, instead of being intimidated, marveled at how He spoke and acted out everything the Father willed, yet they did not recognize His words as His Father's. Furthermore, they were, by nature, hostile and offended towards those words.

Let's look at that closer through an illustration. For example, you have a woman who claims to be married to a man named Jim. Then, a man claiming to be Jim and her husband approaches her. The above case is like the wife doubting this man is her husband. So then, she begins to question him. For example, "If you're Jim, when were you born?" And, "What kind of car did you have when you first got your license?" If he doesn't answer to her satisfaction, she decides that he is not her husband Jim. This might seem reasonable, and if he got the answers incorrect or didn't remember, the people listening might believe her when she says, "this is not my husband."

If there was anybody in the crowd that had wisdom, they might say this begs another question, "Hey lady, are you really Jim's wife or are you an imposter?" The reasoning of the wise man is, do you really need factual evidence to know if he is your husband? Don't you know your husband when he is standing right in front of you? Jesus is marveling at the religious leaders who are supposed to know God and claim to be in union with Him. However, they don't recognize Him when He stands before them. They don't even recognize His words as from God. Do they really need factual evidence to know something that they are supposed to have intimate knowledge of? Next question, why does it not occur to anyone to question if these men of God, leaders of the Jewish faith, may be imposters because they don't judge if someone and their words are from God by their intimate knowledge of God? They need factual evidence?

What did that tell Jesus? It told Him that even the top religious leaders who know the written word by heart can't recognize God when they stand right in front of Him. It told Him that they were, in their inner man, hostile and threatened by God's words. It told Him that, in their inner selves, they really had no love or even any natural attraction towards God, His heart, and the Spirit of His words. They were obviously naturally repelled by them; they had no real love for God and their response showed it. However, to the religious leaders, they thought themselves wise and discerning to hold Jesus and His words suspect by judging Him with factual evidence. How disappointing it must have been to Jesus that the best of the best had no intimate knowledge of God and they were repulsed by Him when facing Him. Yes, Jesus' deduction was correct, there was no love of God in their hearts.

It is a Biblical fact that the major way we will be judged is it will be proven if we have a natural attraction to please God and do His will, therefore saying about us that we love Him more than ourselves. Learning by the folly of the leaders and the scholarly of Jesus' day, it is not by a knowledgeable and scholarly mind that one can successfully judge or discern what words coming from what person are from God or not. You can't judge superficially. No, it takes something much greater than to know every Bible verse by heart and to be able to have insightful knowledge of the person speaking them. It actually takes something much harder to attain than perfect scholarly knowledge of the written word. It takes a pure heart. Not meaning a sinless heart, but one which is single-minded, wanting to please God by serving Him and wanting to do His will at the expense of their own. This is what qualifies one to recognize if something is from God.

WEB Mt 5:8 *Blessed are the pure in heart, for they shall see God.*

It is true that as Colleen and I gain a larger following of our teachings and ministry, people will undoubtedly come to know us personally, and what kind of people we are. However, as teachers, we teach people how to live as spiritual men and women, discerning life in a spiritual way.

We have found the best way to teach discerning of spirit. It is not by knowing how to figure people out or to train them to have a spiritual power. No, we teach them to be single-minded when it comes to God, to be surrendered to His will in a pure or holistic way.

Having a still spirit which is not agitated with passions will create a huge contrast. The contrast of having the stillness of God's Spirit rule your heart coming in contact with the agitated spirit energies the people of this world operate out of makes one sensitive to discern spirit.

Jesus was right; wanting to do God's will with all your heart alone will cause you to recognize if one has God's Spirit in them and if they speak word's which are from God. As the saying goes, "You can't cheat an honest man."

NIV Jn 8:15 You judge by human standards...

NIV Jn 7:24 Stop judging by mere appearances, and make a right judgment."

As such, Colleen and I would like to be known first as a voice, just a voice. We want the words we speak from God to have more prominence and have their own credibility, than that of who we are. Therefore, we don't want to propagate people judging superficially if one is from God by giving our Bio. We want the words we speak to be more important than who we are. We want those who have a pure heart in wanting to serve God to check in their heart if we and the words we speak are from God.

We want those who don't have a pure heart to have a change of heart so they may know for themselves the voice and words of God when they hear them. However, we want to point people in the way to properly discern so they may know for themselves if we are from God and speak His words; in the same way John the Baptist tried to convey. You ask about us, and we will tell you about Him. You insist on wanting to know about us, and we will then tell you, we are just a voice making way for the One you should know and should be asking about. We are not a face or a name or people you should want to know, we are just a voice which gives voice to the One whose words you need to know.

OTHER BOOKS BY THE NAKED APOSTLES

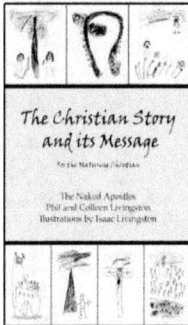

The Christian Story
and its Message

Christianity:
A Lost Civilization

For ordering information please visit our website at
www.nakedapostles.org

OTHER BOOKS BY THE NAKED APOSTLES

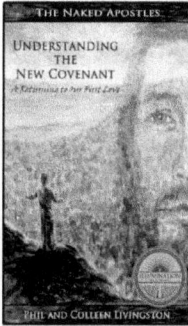

Understanding
the
New Covenant:
*A Returning to Our
First Love*

revelation of Revelation:
*An Urgent Message
for the Church*

Volumes 1-6

For ordering information please visit our website at
www.nakedapostles.org

www.ingramcontent.com/pod-product-compliance
Lightning Source LLC
La Vergne TN
LVHW021403080426
835508LV00020B/2421